Make One Play:
Impact Your Success

Tim Selgo

Make One Play

Impact Your Success

By Tim Selgo

FIVE COUNT
PUBLISHING
LLC

Library of Congress Control Number: Available upon request

Printed and published in the United States by Five Count Publishing LLC.

www.fivecountpub.com.

ISBN (paperback) 978-1-943706-17-4
ISBN (e-book) 978-1-943706-18-1

Cover Design by: Savannah Wells

To my family: Terry, Jenny, Mitch, Rachel, Charlie, Danny, Tray, R.J., Tucker, Henry, and Burke. I hope this husband, father, father-in-law, and grandfather has made at least one play that has helped you in your life.

TABLE OF CONTENTS

GETTING STARTED

"You never know what one play will lead to, fellas."

– Coach Bob Nichols

That's a reminder I heard often as a college basketball player from my coach at the University of Toledo, Bob Nichols. His point was any one play during the course of a game—diving for a loose ball to retain possession, executing the proper screen to free up a shooter, making a hard cut to the basket that shifts the defense and clears the lane for a teammate to score an uncontested layup, anticipating and preventing an opposing player's drive to the basket—could influence the outcome, regardless of when it occurs.

Though the highlights on ESPN's SportsCenter might have you believe otherwise, basketball games aren't always decided by showy dunks and three-pointers, but more often by the plays that lead to them.

Our Toledo team featured a player who demonstrated this concept. Kevin Appel was a six-foot-seven forward who was not all that athletic and did not accumulate much in the way of stats. However, he did a lot of the little things well: set good screens, blocked out in rebounding situations, and was an excellent passer for a big guy. There was one play in particular in an NCAA Tournament game versus Iowa in 1979 when one of our guys missed a free throw and "Apps" reached up and, although he couldn't quite grab the rebound, he got just enough of the ball to tip it out and our team retained possession.

It was at an important part of the game that led us to victory, and Coach Nichols replayed the sequence in our next film session over and over and praised Kevin for a seemingly minor play that did not result in any stats for him. Coach Nichols pointed out that retaining possession led to a score for us, in a game in which we won by only two points, 74-72.

In the more than three decades since my college playing days, I find myself regularly revisiting Coach Nichols' advice. He was trying to win on the courts, of course, but over the years I've realized time and again his strategies apply beyond them as well.

You never know what that one play, that one effort, will

produce. It might be a simple word of encouragement to an employee, a smile for someone having a tough day, or spending twenty to thirty minutes just listening because one of your co-workers wants to be heard. It might be the extra effort that completes a project on time and within budget. Maybe it's you as the role model consistently executing your job so others pattern themselves similarly.

Any one of those simple efforts might be what triggers success for you, your business, or your organization. Successful people understand their importance, and they're always looking for opportunities to extend them. Successful people exemplify the trait of competitive greatness.

In my first book, *Anchor Up: Competitive Greatness the Grand Valley Way*, competitive greatness is defined as coming through with your best effort and best performance when it is most needed.

Our entire lives we have been told to do our best. Our parents have told us that. So have our teachers, coaches, clergy, employers, etc. To do that requires putting forth your best effort every day so your ability to perform will be second nature when the pressure is highest. You are unlikely to just "turn it on" and produce results consistently. You must become accustomed to extending your best effort every day, *because you never know what it will lead to.*

So, how do successful people extend their best effort every day? They master the fundamentals.

That's what this book is about, the fundamentals:

- Have *balance* in your life.
- Surround yourself with the best *people* possible.
- Excel as a *teacher*.
- Have *courage*.
- Be *positive*.
- Be *unselfish* in your pursuits.
- *Commit* to your goals.

These fundamentals will help you regardless of your occupation or position. My career has been in athletics. I started as a basketball student-athlete at the University of Toledo and have spent almost forty years working in college athletics as a coach, administrator, and consultant. Twenty of those years were as the director of athletics at Grand Valley State University, an NCAA Division II school located in Grand Rapids, Michigan, where with the help of a dedicated and committed staff we were able to build perhaps the premier broad-based athletics program in Division II.

In many ways, athletics is like farming—it's not a job, but a way of life. Along the way, athletics has taught me many lessons, including how the proper and consistent execution of the fundamentals is what leads to success. I believe the same holds true in life, both professional and personal.

Why fundamentals? Well, I am a big proponent of keeping things simple. My father was an accomplished teacher and coach at the high school level, and I remember as a kid hearing him refer to the "KISS" principle, which is the acronym for "Keep It Simple, Stupid." I use KISS all the time when I'm speaking to audiences about leadership.

Occasionally there are some well-meaning people who encourage me to soften the adage to "Keep It Simple, Silly" or just plain "Keep It Simple." I respect their concern, but this saying was originated in the U.S. Navy, and my dad—probably the best teacher I've ever known—found it to be a tried-and-true instructional tool. So I'm sticking with "Keep It Simple, Stupid."

Whenever my dad's teams were struggling, he would say it was time to go back to the KISS method of teaching. That meant getting back to the basics, back to the fundamentals, back on track as a team. Return to the foundation of success: the fundamentals.

And they need to be repeated to ensure results. Anyone involved in sports understands repetition. When competing in the toughest of circumstances, you must rely on muscle memory to execute at the highest level. To come through with your best effort and best performance when it is most needed (competitive greatness), you must have repeated that action over and over again in training so you will execute it successfully. The same is true in order to impact your success in anything in life. When you are tested the most, you must rely on the fundamentals of success to come through with your best performance.

In *Anchor Up*, I shared my approach to building and sustaining a great team through personal stories that illustrated my beliefs. This book builds on those stories and adds others from successful people in the business and nonprofit world who were gracious enough to share their thoughts. Many of them are in middle management in some form or another (it probably should be referred to as middle *leadership* rather than middle management), or leaders of small businesses. In some cases they aren't in any leadership position, though I know what they have to say will resonate with you.

Perhaps not every situation is exactly like yours, but most success stories are relatable in many ways. Picture yourself in similar scenarios. Think about what the fundamentals mean in your life and how they can be useful to you. You will see they cross over and blend together in almost every situation. You rarely execute them in isolation, but in combinations. Success in any walk of life requires mastering the fundamentals.

And remember, *you never know what one play will lead to!*

HAVING BALANCE

"The two greatest words in the English language are love and balance."

– John Wooden

H aving balance is the unifying principle that ties all of these concepts of success together. Without balance in your life, it is difficult to achieve lasting success. I have given a lot of talks and presentations in classrooms, business meetings, coaching conventions, and in community settings, and I often promote the balance theme during these speeches. I have some fun with it by using two very famous—and very different—people to talk about being out of balance either in the bad sense or the good sense.

The first slide I show on the screen is a picture of one of the greatest golfers of all time and perhaps one of the greatest competitors of all time: Tiger Woods. The guy was unbelievable for a stretch of about ten years. It seemed as if he would win every tournament he played in, and that the other golfers conceded because they knew Tiger was going to beat them.

I always ask my audience if they know who Tiger Woods is. Most of the time, the answer is yes, regardless of my audience's demographics.

Tiger was the king of golf before his personal life unraveled in 2009. His world careened out of balance probably through a combination of his own doing and the intense public scrutiny the rest of us have never experienced. For the next decade, Woods did not win any major tournaments and was not very competitive since his widely publicized promiscuity and subsequent divorce. I can't profess to know what his life was/is like as perhaps the most celebrated of all celebrities. And I'm not sure what advice I would give to someone like Tiger to try and find some balance in his life, but it was obvious that he needed it.

It is well documented how his father, Earl Woods, trained Tiger from age two to be the best golfer in the world. I don't recommend that for any parent. In fact, I strongly recommend *against* it. Kids are harmed far more than helped by overzealous parents. Anyone who has had children play youth sports knows what I'm talking about. I don't doubt Earl Woods thought he was doing what was best for his son, and they clearly had a great relationship. All I'm saying to you parents is to remember to *find some balance* for your son or daughter.

In an article he wrote for Newsweek in November of 2010 entitled *How I've Redefined Victory*, Tiger said his life was out of balance and his priorities were out of order.

> *Slowly I'm regaining the balance that I'd lost. The healing process is far from complete, but I am beginning to appreciate things I had overlooked before. I'm learning that some victories can mean smiles, not trophies, and that life's most ordinary events can bring joy.*

That was almost a decade ago. In April of 2019, Tiger won the Masters, his first major championship since 2008. Truly this was a moment in sports that will long be remembered, just like many of Tiger's other great accomplishments. But this one was different. The iconic image from the 2019 Masters that everyone saw over and over again after Tiger's victory was not of his famous fist pump or a great shot he made, but rather it was of his little son running up to give his daddy a big hug. Viewers witnessed the sincere, huge smile Tiger had on his face when he saw his boy. Millions watching also broke into huge smiles with genuine happiness for Tiger and his family. He was later awarded the Presidential Medal of Freedom, and I'm sure that was important to Tiger, but it was the smile and hug that seemed to matter more.

It is hard to keep a perfect balance in life, but if your life is going to become unbalanced, make sure it is unbalanced for the *good* things.

That's when I show a slide of Mother Teresa, which usually

gets a chuckle out of my audience. Even if they don't know who Mother Teresa is right away, they just know I'm showing them a nun right after I've shown Tiger Woods, and the juxtaposition is kind of humorous, to say the least.

Then I say Mother Teresa also had her life out of balance. She devoted her life to helping the poor and destitute on the streets of Calcutta, India. That was her calling. The conditions were horrible. Nobody was helping the people there, so she decided she would do something about it. She didn't do it for fame or notoriety, although she was awarded the Nobel Peace Prize in 1979.

To be sure, she followed the fundamentals of being committed, being positive, and being unselfish. She clearly was committed, and she worked hard. She had to remain positive in the worst of conditions, and there is no question she was one of the most unselfish persons of all time. But I doubt if she had much balance in her life in the sense we think of balance. Her calling was such that she didn't have much of a social life or "fun" as we know it. A great portion of her time was spent in helping others, which if you have to be out of balance that at least seems to be a wonderful way to do so.

The point of it all is while people function best when they have some *balance* in life, I am not naïve enough to think it is easily achieved or that there is such a thing as a perfect balance. But if your life is going to get out of balance, make sure it gets out of balance for the good things.

*   *   *   *   *

The successful people mentioned later in this book share some great insights into how they achieve balance in their busy lives. Patti Phillips, CEO of Women Leaders in College Sports, finds balance by staying fit. Both of us practice yoga on occasion as it provides a tremendous workout with balance, and taking care of your own health is important in such a demanding world.

Patti also does not email her leadership team at nights or on weekends. I have heard of CEOs who email and/or call people at all hours of the night, expecting a response. That's ridiculous. That's not leadership, that's the inability to get things done effectively when you are supposed to, at the workplace! Certainly a crisis might necessitate communication at odd hours, but not on a regular basis.

Jim Ayres finds balance in his busy life as managing director of Amway North America by striving to accomplish five things every day. He calls it his Power of 5:

- Read.
- Exercise.
- Learn something new.
- Encourage somebody.
- Be thankful.

Doing all five each day might not be possible for everybody, but Jim's point is having a routine to try to find balance in your life each day will help you achieve success.

Jim says balance means having your priorities straight, and

then some. "It's also acting on those priorities to ensure that whatever I am doing, I am 'all in' and giving one hundred percent energy and focus," Jim said. "For me, it's not about managing my time, it's about managing my energy."

Having your priorities straight will help when problems arise. Early in his career Jim was presented a significant opportunity when his chief operating officer asked him to represent the company and give a presentation at a major conference in Europe. At that point in his career, it was a chance for Jim to gain visibility and responsibility at a much higher level.

Naturally, Jim was excited and put everything he had into being prepared. He was to fly to Europe on a Saturday. But that weekend, one of Jim's children was home from college, and the two went for a walk a few hours before Jim was to head to the airport. On that walk, Jim realized that all was not well. His child was struggling, stressed out, and depressed.

"At that point I knew what I had to do," Jim said. "I had to be a dad. As I returned from the walk, I called my boss and explained that I could not go on the trip. Could there have been career repercussions? Absolutely. But I didn't care. It was a simple decision for me. I didn't stress over it. I didn't analyze it. It was clear what I had to do. I did it. In the end, it all worked out. My weekend at home was important for my child's health. I found a replacement to cover for me in Europe. My management supported me fully. I'm not sure what would have happened had I not had my priorities in place at that moment."

Jim says having balance is critical in the workplace as well. You set the tone for those around you and the whole organization through your actions every day.

"One thing I learned early in my career, which I follow today," Jim said, "is the concept that 'having a bad day is not allowed.' That may sound harsh, but as a leader, it's just reality. Lack of balance leads to bad days."

Jim says he watches for the warning signs that he might be drifting from the center. He said that a few years ago, he was dealing with an issue at home. He was worried, upset, and stressed out by it. During that time, he thought he was able to put it aside at work—until the day a co-worker entered his office and asked if he was angry with her about something.

"I was surprised by the question," Jim said. "Nothing was further from my mind. But instantly I knew I had a problem. I was letting my personal issue impact my demeanor, attitude, and interactions with others. If she felt that way, what was the impact on others? On our morale? Our workplace environment?

"Fortunately, I was able to take that feedback to understand what I was doing, and course correct. It's not easy. But being self-aware and focused on one-hundred-percent positive engagement—in the office, at home and in the community—is essential for anyone aspiring to be a fully functioning successful leader."

Jim Ayres made that one play of being balanced.

* * * * *

John Wooden, the legendary coach of UCLA men's basketball from 1948 to 1975, has influenced me as much as anyone I've ever met. And yes, I did meet this wonderful man, and it was the most enlightening experience in my professional life. (More on that in the next chapter).

In the middle of our visit Wooden said something that has stuck with me—in fact I opened this chapter with it. He said: "The two most important words in the English language are love and *balance.*" He said we all must love and be loved, but we all must try to *achieve a balance* in everything in life. He kept referring to balance, whether the subject was diet, work, rest, family, whatever.

Even when we were talking about something like the fast break Wooden would teach his teams, he said he always wanted the ball to get to the middle of the floor because he wanted the ball handler to be able to go to his left or his right, to *have balance.* He went on to say the hardest offense to defend was one that *had balance.* The team that scored inside and outside, with jump-shooting and with driving the ball to the basket, from the left side of the court and the right side, was the best offensive team. He used that analogy to talk about the importance of balance in life.

Think about your own life. Most people function best when they have some balance in their life, and that's not always easy to achieve. Your family is important, your work is important, your health is important, your spiritual life is important, your social life is important, etc. I don't know about you, but when I neglect one of these areas of my life, not-so-good things tend to happen.

If you're a workaholic, you tend to neglect your family life and health. There's nothing wrong with working hard and being committed to achieving your full potential. After all, I stress that as a fundamental in this book. But you *must have balance* in your life to truly reach your full potential.

In addition to John Wooden, I gained a lot of insight from John Savage, a giant in the life insurance industry, a highly sought-after speaker, and a University of Toledo supporter who I knew well and respected. He had a couple of sayings that illustrate the kind of balance I'm talking about. One is: "Work eight hours, sleep eight hours—just don't confuse the two." That's a great one! Yes, hard work is vital to success in anything. But if you don't get the proper rest, you'll be burned out. If you rest too much or become lazy, you won't accomplish anything.

Another great saying of John's was, "If you are in a boat on Lake Erie and a storm comes up, pray to God but row to shore!" In other words, your spiritual life is important, but you must also do the work necessary to be successful in any endeavor.

* * * * *

A great book to read on this is *Calming the Storm Within* by Jim Lange. Jim is a fellow University of Toledo basketball alum and does a great job offering advice on finding that peace of mind we all seek. In order to become the best you are capable of becoming, you have to find time to quiet the storm of daily life in the twenty-first century.

Another great book is *Quiet, the Power of Introverts in a World That Can't Stop Talking* by Susan Cain. Even after reading the book, I can't tell if I'm an introvert or extrovert. I think I'm a combination, as I suspect most people are. I really love the title of this wonderful book. A "world that can't stop talking" describes our culture very well. In today's media-driven society, there is "noise" around us all the time.

Next time you hop in the car, keep the radio turned off and just think (while watching the road of course!). As Jim Lange suggests in his book, and others have as well, driving offers a time to be by yourself and think. It's also a good time for prayer, regardless of your faith. Try it. You'll be amazed at the balance it brings to your being.

Another way I find time for peace and quiet in my life is by going for walks. Walking is great exercise and it gives one time to think. You can experience nature, gain some quiet in a world that never stops talking, and do some good-old plain thinking. Hiking in a new area is also great exercise, but more importantly, being in a new area can help take your mind off of the daily stresses of life.

You might have other ways of finding balance. The point is to find something that helps balance a world that never stops being busy.

To be sure, the hustle and bustle of daily life can wear you down. We all have responsibilities that weigh on us heavily at times. I believe to achieve one's full potential, you must *strive for balance* in anything you do. Finding a perfect balance is hard to achieve and probably impossible. But if your life becomes out of balance, make sure it's for the *good* things. Following the fundamentals in this book can help us be the best we are capable of becoming. But in my mind, there is no question you have to *have balance* in your life.

You never know what being balanced will lead to!

PEOPLE MAKE YOU SUCCESSFUL

"You lead people and manage things."

– John Savage

J ohn Savage was fond of coining sayings and phrases to make a point, and he certainly was spot-on with the quote above. Regardless of whatever widget or service your company produces or provides, *people* make you successful. Successful people understand developing and maintaining meaningful and trusting relationships with others is essential.

John Savage understood that. So did John Wooden. In 2005, I and seven others visited the coach I revered as a role model from the time I was a kid. And if you think John Wooden lived extravagantly, think again. Here he was in a modest two-bedroom apartment in Encino, California, that resembled what most of us occupied during our college years more than a residence for the greatest coach in any sport at any level. And as his surroundings suggested, Wooden himself was a humble man who welcomed the opportunity to share his thoughts on success for about three hours with eight people he'd never even met.

At the end of our session, we asked if he'd be willing to take a few photos with us and sign some memorabilia. Wooden graciously spent the next half hour doing so. I was smart enough to remember to bring with me *They Call Me Coach*, the first book written about Wooden, published in 1972. I was in the eighth grade when I first read it, and I have re-read it at least five times since. Having Coach Wooden's personal signature in that book makes it a treasure in my library.

With us on that visit was Chuck Martin, our head football coach at Grand Valley State who would later become the head coach at Miami of Ohio. Chuck didn't have anything to sign, but Wooden had two stacks of photos incorporating his *Pyramid of Success*, something Wooden came up with to define success by using the building blocks of a pyramid. There were two versions of the promotional photo: one of the pyramid with a picture of Wooden as the UCLA coach in his suit and tie with his signature rolled-up program in his hands, and the other of the pyramid with a picture of Wooden from his earlier years with a whistle around his neck standing in front of a chalkboard with a play diagram scribbled on it.

Wooden started to sign the more modern of the two before he paused and peered at Chuck. "Wait a minute," he said. "I want to sign this other one for you, and in a minute I will tell you why."

It did take about a minute for the elderly gentleman to scribe his name on the photo. Then Wooden asked if Chuck recognized the diagram on the blackboard. Without hesitation, he acknowledged it was Coach Wooden's famous 2-2-1 zone press.

But it was different than most coaches' diagrams. There were the typical "O's" representing the players on offense, but instead of "X's" for the defense, there were the actual names of the players on Wooden's UCLA team at the time (including hall-of-famers Walt Hazzard, Gail Goodrich, and Keith Erickson, who in addition to his basketball accomplishments was selected to play on the 1964 U.S. Olympic *Volleyball* team!).

As Wooden handed Chuck the signed pyramid photo, he said, "I wanted you to have this one because I ran that press for a lot of years, but it worked a lot better when I had those guys!"

The emphasis on people was a recurring theme throughout the visit. Wooden often made references like, "Now, you must have the talent to win a championship," or in his generation's vernacular, "You must have the material to be highly successful."

This is a coach who won more than eighty percent of his games and ten national championships telling us it's about people. *People* made that press successful. Yes, it was a good strategy, but *people* made it work.

As we were flying home, the leader of our expedition asked me and Chuck to state our most important takeaway from meeting with Coach Wooden. Immediately and simultaneously we replied: "You have to have the talent to be successful!"

Yes, the greatest coach in my lifetime made it clear to us that success comes from the people you surround yourself with.

Wooden's principles of success are timeless. Among resources we provided to student-athletes who participated in our leadership development program at Grand Valley State was the book *A Lifetime of Observations and Reflections On and Off the Court*, written by Coach Wooden and Steve Jamison. I would tell our students that while Wooden carved out his coaching success long before they were born, his principles span generations.

That was confirmed to me one day when Gabrielle Shipley, our star golfer who won the NCAA Division II national championship in 2016 approached me and said, "Mr. Selgo, this book is awesome! I learned so much from it and just wanted to thank you for giving it to us."

You don't have to be in sports to benefit from Wooden's principles of success, either. I highly encourage everyone to read books by and about John Wooden. You won't have any trouble finding them—dozens have been published either by him or about his leadership theories. I guarantee they will help you achieve success whether you are a leader or not.

* * * * *

Another legendary coach who understood the people principle is Bill Walsh, who led his San Francisco 49ers to three Super Bowl championships in the NFL. In his autobiography, *Building a Champion,* Walsh offers a critical piece of advice for us all: Make it a study of people.

From the time he began his career in coaching, Walsh desperately wanted to be a head coach in the NFL, but he spent numerous years as an assistant before Stanford University hired him as head coach in the college ranks. After two years in Palo Alto, Walsh finally realized his dream by being named head coach of the 49ers. (Though it could have been a nightmare; at the time the 49ers were the worst franchise in the NFL.)

Walsh offers insight into his success by replaying his first day on the job:

> *I can distinctly recall driving to the 49er training facility in Redwood City for the first time. I readied myself for the seemingly awesome responsibilities I had just taken on. I reflected on the years I had waited in frustration for this opportunity. Fortunately, as it turned out, I had been gaining invaluable experience. I was*

> *self-assured and confident and, for the first time, appreciated those years. As I parked and headed for the entrance, I reminded myself to have patience, let others do much of the talking, make this a study of people, and that it was going to take time.*

Remember, this is a guy who went on to win three Super Bowls and produce a number of hall of famers. The media dubbed him "The Genius" because he developed and perfected the West Coast Offense, which deployed running backs and tight ends in a ball-control passing game that was almost impossible to stop because it was so unique.

He didn't say, "Let's go design the fanciest plays," or "Let's out-scheme everybody in professional football." No, he said, "Make it a study of people."

Walsh understood success in football was about people. Walsh knew finding the right people for his organization and developing them to the best of his ability was the key to success in the NFL, and that holds true for any business or profession. Again, it doesn't matter what widget or service you are providing: People make you successful.

Later in his autobiography Walsh talks about drafting a guy named Jerry Rice. Yes, the same Jerry Rice who went on to become arguably the best receiver to ever play the game. Walsh had heard about this kid setting all kinds of NCAA records at Mississippi Valley State and wanted to check him out. One Saturday night when the 49ers were in Houston for a game with the Oilers the next day, Walsh was watching sports highlights on the local news as he was dozing, and Rice grabbed his attention. Rice's 40-yard-dash times were not overly impressive, and in fact, one 49ers scout felt he was no better than a sixth-round pick. But Walsh saw that he had "functional speed," meaning when he had the ball he ran as fast as he did without it and defenders did not catch him. Walsh saw Rice was more than just a guy who could catch passes. He saw a player who competed hard on every play. When Walsh convinced his staff Rice was one of the most competitive individuals the 49ers had ever scouted, they drafted him in the first round.

Jerry Rice's individual workout programs are legendary in the football world. The lengths he would go to improve as a player are well documented. Walsh discovered that by studying Rice as a person, not simply as a football player. The guy had unbelievable competitive juices, and Walsh wanted that on his team.

Walsh also drafted a player named Joe Montana, one of the most accomplished NFL quarterbacks of all-time who many teams ignored on draft day because they thought he had a slight frame and he did not possess enough arm strength. Not Walsh. He examined Montana the person and besides having quick feet and a quick throwing delivery, he couldn't help but notice how he had led Notre Dame to multiple come-from-behind victories in the fourth quarter during his senior season alone, including leading the Irish to three touchdowns in the last eight minutes to win the Cotton Bowl. During his NFL career, he led his teams to 32 fourth-quarter come-from-behind victories!

Montana maintained poise under pressure and thus achieved his best performance when it was most needed (competitive greatness!). That told Walsh Montana understood the need to repeat the fundamentals to the point at which his best performance was second nature. Walsh made it a study of people, not just football talent.

*   *   *   *   *

Even our U.S. presidents must rely on people to succeed (or at least they should know better). In Donald T. Phillips' book *Lincoln on Leadership*, this passage describes how one of our country's greatest presidents emphasized people as a leader:

> *Lincoln gained commitment and respect from his people because he was willing to take time out from his busy schedule to hear what his people had to say. It's no different when you're running a business. If you stay in touch with the people who comprise the foundation, you're more likely to gain an advantage that helps you to win the war against stiff competition. It's the people who are closest to the consumer and the product who know how to win. And, almost always, they will want to offer their ideas.*

Lincoln understood people were the key to success during one of our country's most challenging times. Late in the Civil War, Lincoln was becoming frustrated with his staff (has that ever happened to you?). General George McClellan was not being aggressive enough and wasn't taking action, and Lincoln, back in the White House, couldn't understand why. So what did he do? He rode by horseback to the frontlines and spoke with Union Army officers who corroborated Lincoln's disappointment. They complained McClellan was timid and sluggish and couldn't decide, a key component in leadership. There comes a time when you have gathered all of the collaborative thoughts and ideas of your staff, and as the leader, you must decide and take action. McClellan's staff, and Lincoln, had lost confidence in him, so Lincoln is the one who decided. He fired McClellan and replaced him with General Ambrose Burnside, and the rest, as they say, is history.

Lincoln made a critical decision that turned the Civil War in the Union Army's favor because he studied his people. Winning the war depended largely on weaponry and resources. The Union Army had the upper hand in both but the wrong general. People were the difference. Lincoln put the right person in place and the Union prevailed.

* * * * *

The need to emphasize people hit home with me on a local scale recently when visiting with Steve Paine, the president of Fab-Lite, a small, family-owned manufacturing company of office furniture in Manistee, Michigan. He was showing me around his plant and introducing me to his employees. It was evident they respected him, they appreciated his leadership, and they enjoyed working there.

While walking me up the stairs to his office and describing everything they do, Steve said, "You gotta love the people!"

Steve may be president of the company, but he knows good and well that people make his business successful. Yes, they have a fine product, and yes, they deploy sound processes and operations to be effective, but in order to achieve desired outcomes, the people at Fab-Lite are what make the difference.

Steve loves and appreciates the people under his umbrella. In turn, they love and appreciate working there. No place is perfect, but in every successful business that has stood the test of time, you'll find leaders appreciate their people and understand if they help their employees become successful, they in turn will achieve success. Successful leadership is about people, not products. Remember, you lead people and manage things.

As president of Fab-lite, Steve goes to great lengths to develop the people who work there to become leaders. Manistee is in a beautiful part of Michigan but a long way from any metropolitan area. Their location makes it tough to attract engineers and fill other highly skilled positions. Their supply of people may be a limitation, but the company does not use that as an excuse. They still make it a study of people—finding the right fit with people who want to live there and contribute to community success.

Since its humble beginnings in 1984, Fab-lite has grown from a company of ten employees to eighty. More than seventy percent of the supervisors are the result of promotion from within, a good number of them having been hourly employees who learned the leadership skills necessary to make them effective managers. In the past thirty-five years, Fab-Lite's annual sales have increased from $1 million to more than $20 million. Despite their limitations, this company is a great success and has developed its people from within to become a pillar in their community.

Your business or organization probably has limitations as well. All do. If you are the leader, it is your job to find a way to be successful anyway. In some cases, perhaps the current people are the problem. What if you became the leader of the organization and discovered your work force was hindering your success? In those instances, it may take several years to get the right people in place, but that has to be your first order of business. The top priority for leaders is surrounding themselves with the best people possible.

Even if you are not in a leadership position with an organization, or you are self-employed or a sole practitioner, align yourself with people/colleagues/business cohorts you can lean on professionally and personally for advice and friendship. In other words, surround yourself with people you can trust. Your chances of success will increase greatly!

Occasionally, there may be some people who just aren't going to fit within your organization and you have to make a change. You may find you just cannot be compatible with your fellow workers for some good reason. Perhaps you just cannot do business with someone because of a difference in values. More often than not, though, wholesale changes tend to be a mistake. "Change agents" often discover they cannot hire people better than the ones they already have.

People need developing, just like whatever widget or service you are providing. Everybody has their strengths and weaknesses. Work hard to identify the hidden talents of those you interact with, and then use them to construct stronger personal and professional relationships. Usually it just takes time to make a relationship successful.

A great example of this is the career of Mike Krzyzewski, the famous Duke University head men's basketball coach. He posted an unimpressive 38-47 record in his first three years at Duke, and despite rumblings from boosters and alumni calling for a change, Athletics Director Tom Butters saw talent there and stuck with Coach K. Of course, Coach K has gone on to be Duke's head coach for thirty-eight years and counting, winning five national championships along with more than a dozen Atlantic Coast Conference regular-season and tournament titles. In addition, he has developed his players at a prolific level, producing 41 first-round picks as of 2019 in the NBA draft, more than any other coach in history.

It is a good thing for Duke Tom Butters committed to Coach K. *(You never know what it will lead to!)*

Invest your time, money, and energy in people. Make it the highest priority for your company to hire and train the right people. In my first book, *Anchor Up*, I go into great detail about what's necessary to hire the best people possible. None of the other fundamentals for success matter unless you surround yourself with the best people possible and help them become the best they can be. If you do that, you will find success.

After the 2002 Grand Valley State University women's soccer season, we embarked on a search for a new head coach and committed to making the position full time rather than the part-time job it had always been before. Our record in women's soccer was only 56-57-5 since we began the sport in 1996, and it was time to make this program more successful. As the search committee was sifting through the applicants, I kept returning to one résumé from a high school coach named Dave DiIanni. Dave had been the head girls coach at Jackson Lumen Christi High School in Michigan and had great success there. I noted the number of championships his team had won and that they had consistently finished in the top ten in the state. This guy had built a program, not a one-hit wonder: He was a long-term thinker who wanted to build something that would last. That was exactly what I wanted.

A short-term thinking, transactional leader will almost certainly lead an organization down the wrong path. The best leaders put their companies, units, or teams in a position to succeed even after they are no longer there.

In the search committee meeting we narrowed the candidates down to those we wanted to interview. Nobody else had Dave in their top choices. Based on his track record, I insisted we bring him in for an interview. I didn't care if he was "only" a high school coach. This guy was a winner.

Five minutes into the interview I jotted down on my notepad: "This guy can really teach his sport." I knew we had found our next head coach. Dave went on to establish a record of 221-18-18 over eleven seasons at Grand Valley while winning three national championships. He then was named the head coach at the University of Iowa and is doing a great job there in building that program for the long haul. In the interview, Dave talked at length about the kind of player he was going to recruit and how he was going to develop them as leaders. Although he talked about strategy, it was clear how he was going to make us a winner. People make you successful!

My overall approach to hiring is that you are better off erring on the side of interviewing more rather than fewer candidates. I often wonder what would have happened if I hadn't insisted on bringing Dave in for an interview.

You never know what surrounding yourself with the right people will lead to!

TEACH

"Good teachers know how to bring out the best in students."

– Charles Kuralt

Likewise, successful leaders bring out the best in those they are leading. Given that, I would argue the best leaders are those who are the best teachers. All of the great leaders I have studied were great teachers. They taught those under them how to be the best they could be. That is how they found success!

If you don't find yourself in a leadership position, seek out those you report to as an opportunity to continue your professional growth and learning so you can eventually reach a position of leadership. At the very least you will have a better understanding of your role in the business/organization, and how you can help it move forward and achieve success. Whether you are a leader or not, you do have a role in your organization—often a teaching role. Perhaps you have to teach your co-workers, or even at times your supervisors. Your ability to be a good teacher will be a magnet in drawing good people to your area of the organization. People *want* to be taught, so regardless of your position, seek improvement in the teaching skills described below and you will achieve greater success.

I grew up in a household of teachers. My father was an outstanding history and geography teacher (before it became social studies). He also was a highly successful high school basketball coach. Why? Because he could teach the game of basketball to his students, his players. And I began my career as a math teacher at the high school level. If you want to be successful, learn to teach!

Whenever I speak to any group on leadership, I conduct a short exercise to demonstrate how the best leaders are great teachers. I ask them to think of the best teacher they ever had.

You should try it yourself. Go ahead, think of the best teacher in your lifetime. It could be a grade school, high school, or college teacher, a coach, a parent, a member of the clergy, a boss, anyone. Who immediately pops into your head?

Now I want you to close your eyes (after reading the following instructions, of course). Take ten seconds. Then answer this question: What is the trait (or traits) this person possessed that caused him or her to pop into your head as the best teacher you ever had?

The responses are almost always the same. They include:

- She cared.
- He kept me accountable.
- She was enthusiastic.
- He took a personal interest in me and listened.
- She challenged me.
- He knew his stuff.
- She was positive.
- He took the time to help me.
- She explained things well.
- He clearly cared about his students more than his own personal gain in life.
- She sacrificed her time for her students.
- He cared about me as a person and not just as a student or a player.
- She was inspiring.

I could add more, but you get the idea. After listing their responses on the board, I look at the attendees and tell them that if they want to be successful, do those things! Teach!

* * * * *

Great teachers use repetition in teaching any subject. Repetition also leads to consistency. All the great leaders I have studied share consistency as a defining characteristic. As you develop a core set of behaviors that define you, repeat them consistently to achieve success.

Jim Ayres, mentioned in the Balance chapter, is managing director of Amway North America, a division of Amway, an American company specializing in health, beauty, and home care products. Amway is composed of people who own their own businesses, so Jim's job is to help them operate those businesses as successfully as possible. He makes several presentations to these owners and always uses the following guidelines:

- Tell them what you are going to tell them.
- Tell them.
- Tell them what you told them.

Yes, it is repetitive, but that is part of driving home the fundamentals to your people so doing their jobs becomes second nature.

Jim's approach saw Amway North America experience growth in three of four years even though sales for the company overall increased only one year during the same period. As Managing Director, Jim's strategies have generated a growth rate nearly eight percentage points higher than the parent company. In addition to increasing sales, Amway North America also doubled in profitability over the same stretch.

Jim does something else I appreciate. In his college days, Jim was an offensive lineman at Grand Valley State University, where I was the director of athletics from 1996 through 2016. Jim became accustomed to repetition as a highly skilled athlete, and he has an interesting take on it today. He routinely asks people: "What's your six-inch jab step?"

What does he mean by that? Well, as an offensive lineman, it's critical to have the right footwork. Jim was up against big defensive ends and speedy linebackers coming at him from every angle, and he had to maintain his balance to react whichever way they moved in order to block them. That's why a "six-inch jab step" was so important, and why it needed to be repeated so consistently in practice. It had to be six inches to maintain the right balance, not five, not seven, but *six*, and they practiced it *every day.*

And what did repetition do for him and his teammates? Well, Grand Valley State, an NCAA Division II school, has built the winningest football program in the nation at any level thanks to the commitment to teaching by its coaches.

It's the same with any form of success. Some things you must practice *every day.* Here's what Jim does before every meeting: He starts by recognizing someone for their good work. Who doesn't like that? Positive recognition is among the best motivational tools out there. Employees and the teams they are a part of perform better when they're recognized for their efforts. *(And you never know what one effort will lead to!)* Jim makes that a habit. That's repetition of successful leadership.

Every profession has a professional organization from which members can learn as well. Leaders (i.e., good teachers) must encourage their employees to seek additional learning experiences for professional and personal growth. Not all teaching has to come directly from leadership, but employees should be encouraged to learn through their professional associations as well. If your boss doesn't encourage this, find ways to develop professionally anyway. Successful people do that!

For me, during my career as a director of athletics at the collegiate level, I learned about leadership as a member of the National Association of Collegiate Directors of Athletics (NACDA). After attending our convention for several years, I was appointed to the Executive Committee and later became an officer with NACDA and eventually the president in 2015-16. From these experiences I was able to watch and learn from some of the most successful people in my profession, which is often the simplest and most effective way to learn, keep improving, and find success in whatever you do.

If you are going to be the best teacher—the best leader—you can be, you need to be a continuous learner as well. Successful people operate that way. I harken back to a saying posted in the locker room during my college basketball days: "When you're through improving, you're through!" You should make it a point to lead by example. Show your staff that you're constantly learning how to improve.

* * * * *

In the last chapter I advised you to read any book you can find about John Wooden's leadership principles. Here's one I like in particular by Swen Nater and Ronald Gallimore: *You Haven't Taught Until They Have Learned: John Wooden's Teaching Principles and Practices.*

The book describes how John Wooden taught. It doesn't offer the great plays Wooden designed or the magical offenses and defenses he deployed. Rather, Nater explains how Wooden *taught* them—how he implored his players to understand and learn and succeed. Wooden was highly successful because he could communicate as a teacher.

Nater played at UCLA for Wooden but was a backup his entire career there to Bill Walton, a Hall of Famer. Gallimore and a colleague watched every UCLA practice throughout the 1974-75 season and recorded Coach Wooden's acts of teaching. Following this, Gallimore and his colleague concluded *"that his teaching practices illustrated what research showed to be effective teaching (i.e., well planned, brisk lessons that are information-rich and engaging.)"* Those of you who lead meetings at your place of work take heed. Plan your meetings so they are *"brisk, information-rich and engaging."*

Nater goes on to illustrate a teaching/leadership lesson Coach Wooden taught him, and it applies to every leader. Again, Nater rarely played at UCLA because he was Bill Walton's backup, but that didn't mean Coach Wooden didn't care as much about him as he did every other player on the team. Here are some thoughts Nater shares in the book and a specific example he provides:

> *When I joined the UCLA team, at first I thought I sensed an equal opportunity. But that feeling did not last long. My more talented and experienced teammates became "regulars" while the rest of us became members of the supporting cast—the reserves.*

But Coach Wooden knew he would need the reserves at some point in the season, and he intended to let them know they were essential. He constantly felt compelled to make that point and described that it took a "special effort to make sure we do have harmony in the group as a whole."

Nater describes an example of this during his senior year when he was, once again, a reserve who didn't play until the game was essentially decided:

> *During a road game in Pullman, Washington, near the end of league play, the contest had been decided and I entered the game with two minutes to play. Two minutes. That's not even enough time to get tired! One of the Cougars missed a shot and I grabbed the rebound. Andy Hill, one of my teammates, quickly cut to the corner to receive my outlet pass. It was just as we practiced. My pass to him would start the fast break to the other end of the court. But a strange thought entered my head. "If I pass Andy the ball, I'll probably (no certainly) never see it again." So I decided to keep the ball and dribble down the court like a guard. What did I have to lose?*

He shared that the game was on national television and that fans today from all over the country remind him of what happened next.

> *From the UCLA bench Coach Wooden yelled, and the microphones easily picked it up, "Swen, you are not to dribble the ball!"*

Of course Nater passed the ball to Hill. Even in a game in which the outcome was already decided, Coach Wooden demonstrated he cared about Swen enough to keep teaching. He cared about his development and Swen never forgot it. He went on to be the first player ever drafted in the NBA's first round without ever starting a game in college, a tribute to the way Coach Wooden could teach and develop his players.

Another point to be made here is that Nater *learned* what Wooden *taught.* Nater learned from him. He was coachable. Frankly, a prerequisite to being a good teacher is to be a good learner. Learn from good teachers. You may never be in a leadership position, but you will become more successful if you are willing to be taught and are willing to learn. As time goes by, you will become a better teacher and will find more success.

I also told you in the last chapter how much being able to visit Coach Wooden in person meant to me. One other thing that stood out in that meeting was how often Wooden used the word "teach." It must have been more than twenty-five times. Perhaps it was so obvious to me because I hardly ever hear people say "teach" anymore. When was the last time you heard a leader use it?

When I asked Steve Paine, the president of Fab-Lite, about how much teaching he does as a leader, his eyes sparkled and he said, "Plenty. Our shop workers make office furniture, and each manager must be taught how that is done because there is turnover in these positions and they must be able to teach the next person. Hourly workers often become supervisors who pass on to their successors the skills necessary to make the product."

In other words, the hourly workers become teachers. Steve is developing an entire workforce to become better at teaching. It is not surprising they are achieving great success as a company.

Steve talked about the kind of person he looks for in a supervisor on the shop floor. For him, the candidate must satisfy these two conditions:

- Do they exhibit a strong work ethic?
- Do they have the attitude sufficient to remain poised and solve problems?

There you go. It's not complicated. (KISS!) Steve said if they possess those two ingredients he can work with them and teach them the business, and they in turn can become successful.

I always felt when hiring people you should start with whether they are hard workers and if they are good people—then we'll look for other things. I explained earlier about surrounding yourself with the right people to become successful. Steve Paine is also telling you to become a good teacher, no matter your role in the organization.

* * * * *

Successful teaching requires effective communication. In

today's world, communication occurs in many forms: in person, over the phone, via email or text, etc. I would often tell my staff to *over-communicate*. Never assume people understand you. As the title of Swen Nater's book about Wooden says, "you haven't taught until they have learned." In other terms, you haven't communicated well until those receiving the message completely understand what you are saying.

Women Leaders in College Sports, mentioned in the Balance chapter, is a nonprofit organization whose mission is developing, connecting, and advancing women in leadership positions in college athletics. As the head of a staff of eleven, CEO Patti Phillips describes herself as a coach. "I lead as a coach and I teach as a coach, which means I give constant feedback," she said.

I couldn't agree more. The successful coaches—the successful teachers—provide feedback consistently. Sometimes it might be constructive criticism. As Patti says, "When I correct them, it's because as a coach, I want them to improve." A lot of coaches have become successful in other professions because they can teach.

Father Jim Bacik is a Catholic priest of the Diocese of Toledo who earned his doctorate in theology from the University of Oxford and has published many articles and books. He is easily one of the five smartest people I have ever known. He has the wonderful gift of explaining things simply so non-theologians like me can understand them.

Once while we were having lunch together and I was sharing some of my experiences with my own children, he taught me a simple yet valuable lesson about parenting. He didn't get all psychological about it, either. He simply said, "My mother had a wonderful gift—she accepted all of her children *as we were.*" This made me think about my children and how different each one was. Sure, I wanted them to learn to exhibit their best behavior, but I also had to be willing to accept they each had their own personality and it was me, the parent, who had to adapt to their personality. The same is true for leading or working with people: Accept them as they are and then teach them with the best method possible given their personalities.

Similarly, the best lawyers and accountants are those who can explain their complex legal terms or accounting methods in ways others can understand. In other words, successful lawyers and accountants are those who can *teach* their clients.

Mike Spiros has operated his own law practice for forty-six years and has taught paralegal studies at the University of Toledo for more than thirty-seven years. Whenever I've needed legal services from Mike, he's always done a great job of explaining terms in words and phrases I can understand. That is teaching. Mike is able to summarize most of it in layman's terms so his clients understand the legalese. He teaches his clients what they must know. He leads them in solving their problems.

As a professor who spends most of his days in his office dealing with real-life legal situations, Mike shares his experiences with his students. He teaches them what "real life" as a lawyer is. He continually receives high marks in student evaluations, the true measure of an excellent teacher. And he understands the importance of motivation and inspiration in teaching.

Mike told me he once had a thirty-five-year-old non-traditional student in one of his classes. She was a single parent of two children paying her own way through college, and she did not believe going on to law school and becoming a lawyer was possible for her. Mike challenged her on that because she was a really good student who was certainly capable of succeeding there. Her thought process was that she was thirty-five, she had to work to support her two children, and it would take five years for her to complete law school because she would have to attend part time. Mike's reply was, "You are going to turn forty in five years no matter what happens. The question is, do you want to be a forty-year-old paralegal or a forty-year-old lawyer?" A few years later Mike ran into her and she reminded him of what he had told her. And she was now a lawyer! *You never know what one word of encouragement will lead to!*

When was the last time you inspired someone on your staff or a co-worker to think bigger and challenged them to not settle for their current position? If they have talent, as Mike's student did, be a teacher. Motivate them. Show them the way. That's developing your people. That's impacting your success!

*   *   *   *   *

You'll note in the characteristics of great teachers listed earlier in this chapter, a common theme is them taking a genuine interest in their pupils, which is demonstrated in the way they listen. Successful leaders are like great teachers. They genuinely listen to people.

In his book, *A Higher Loyalty; Truth, Lies, and Leadership*, former FBI director James Comey describes former President Barack Obama's listening skills as follows:

> *Obama had the ability to really discuss something, leveling the field to draw out perspectives different from his own. He would turn and face the speaker, giving them long periods without interruption to share their view. And although he was quiet, he was using his face, his posture, and sometimes small sounds to draw the person out. He was carefully tracking what they said, something he would prove by asking questions when they were finished; the questions were often drawn from throughout the minutes he had been listening.*

Obviously, President Obama genuinely listened to Comey to make such an impactful impression. The best teachers can do that as well. Their entire focus is on you when you are speaking. They then ask the right questions or make a point to add to the teaching moment. If you want to be successful, discipline yourself to listen the way President Obama listens.

Genuine listening develops trust. Those you are working with will trust you more if they know you listen to them, even if you do not take action as they would like. And you will learn to trust your co-workers better when you truly listen to what they have to say, even if you may disagree with them. You learn to see all perspectives of a situation and thus make better decisions. By listening in a genuine way, you are being a successful teacher.

Do you want to be successful? Then work at being a good teacher! Revisit the traits listed in the beginning of this chapter and focus on accomplishing as many as you can.

You never know what one teaching moment will lead to!

COURAGE

"Success is not final, failure is not fatal: It is the courage to continue that counts."

– Winston Churchill

E ntrepreneur Doug LaFleur started a data analytics company for school districts called Eidex, which provides research-based tools that empower district leaders to focus on areas of need, improve decision-making, and save time. He now runs it with his business partner, Jack Gunn.

Starting a business involves risk, and risk can be scary. That's when courage is required. All successful people must have courage and believe in what they are doing.

Doug's entrepreneurial spirit emerges when he discusses the

courage it takes to lead a new business. "Many business entrepreneurs have a mix of courage, strong confidence in their abilities, and optimism about the future," he said. "But once the excitement of the new endeavor wears off, a business owner also has to become comfortable with being uncomfortable, and I have lived by that mantra most of my life."

Doug launched Eidex when he was in his early fifties, and he took significant risk in doing so. He sold interest in another business and used it to fund Eidex and live on for a few years while the new endeavor grew enough to attract investors. There have been times when he and Jack have not taken a salary, or they've had to adjust their salaries dramatically in order to keep the business moving forward.

"This can take courage to keep believing in the vision and keep building and selling," Doug said. "Where it gets real tough, and where the need for courage really kicks in, is when the industry you are in continues to evolve—and it always does—and you realize that the business model you started with may need to change in order for the business to be sustainable."

As Doug says, that can be extremely unsettling. Every business is ever-changing, and market needs continue to adjust over time. Plus, your competitors are all trying to change and adapt at the same time.

"Courage is showing up the next day, even if you feel distraught and discouraged, and keeping a smile on the outside while having a feeling of unease and insecurity on the inside,"

Doug said. "Then, courage is making decisions that you are pretty sure will work, but you are not positive will work, and then putting your head down and focusing on the new strategy, while exhibiting an optimistic persona to your staff.

"It is also knowing that a change in strategy may not see results overnight, and keeping your optimism and enthusiasm up while methodically working on a new direction. If courage is strength in the face of pain or grief, then in my humble opinion, courage is something a new business owner needs to have in abundance."

How do they deal with the challenges of building a company? Doug says, "We just keep working. We believe if we have perseverance that things will work out. It doesn't need to be more complicated than that." (KISS!)

And build a successful company they have. Eidex has remained in business since 2011 and has doubled its workforce during that time in order to keep up with the demand for their services. The courage of their conviction has led them to continue forward with an entrepreneurial spirit and has benefitted many school systems over the years.

Likewise, Mike Spiros, the lawyer mentioned in the previous chapter on teaching, describes the courage it took for him to practice law on his own:

"I had a partner for the first nineteen years of my practice who decided to leave on short notice. I had never practiced entirely on my own and was faced with the prospect of handling high overhead and having to buy him out of not only his share of the practice but also of the office building that we owned together—all this while maintaining my teaching schedule and work I was doing as a statistician for the University of Toledo basketball team.

"The temptation was to give up teaching and/or the work with the basketball program, both of which I had a passion for, or scale way back on the practice, which would be difficult because of the fixed nature of the overhead. What I did lacked drama or maybe anything worth writing about. I just decided to square my shoulders and continue on, put one foot in front of the other and not feel sorry for myself.

"It turned out quite well. Perhaps, without being told explicitly, I had picked up the message that you're going to face adversity at some point and how you handle it will have a lot to do with your success or lack thereof. The truth, though, is that I didn't think of it that way at the time. No pep talk, no 'you can do it,' I just got up every morning and went about my business. Eventually I acquired another partner who has been with me ever since, and here we are."

Many of you reading this are probably small-business owners with a small staff and can relate to Mike's story. There was no fanfare, no pep talks, no board to provide advice or guidance, just his own will and courage to keep getting up every day and practicing law. Even though there may be only a limited staff around you on a daily basis, it is a story of courage. It is a story of success! You don't have to influence hundreds of people to make an impact. Just keep getting up every day. Others will take notice, and you never know the positive influence you may have on them. People will recognize the courage it takes to start your own business, and as Mike said, square your shoulders, put one foot in front of the other, and keep going.

The Texas Rangers of the Old West had a saying: "There's no stopping a man who knows he's in the right and keeps on a-coming!" The leaders at Eidex believe they are doing something positive for education and are making an impact. Think about the hundreds of people who have benefitted over the years from Mike Spiro's legal work because of that one play of going out on his own. They know they are doing something right and they keep on a-coming.

* * * * *

Agropur is a North American dairy industry headquartered in Saint-Hubert, Quebec, Canada. A few years ago, its Grand Rapids, Michigan, production plant was struggling, having lost more than $10 million in the previous fiscal year. All but a handful of the management team turned over. The new plant manager, Jim Mick, met with the remaining staff on day one and told them his vision and his goals for this facility. He was clear and handed out a sheet of paper to everyone in the room with goals and the deadlines by which to accomplish them. Then he said the words of a person who had been successful before, someone who is a successful leader: "Today is a new day. I need everyone in this room to commit one-hundred percent to these goals. If you have any doubt, I will personally find you another career path because this is not going to work. It is time to roll up our sleeves, get back to basics and cut out the low-hanging fruit. We are going to win, starting right now!"

There was a lot of changeover during this time. The management staff averaged sixty hours of work each week. Not once were they told this was what they had to do, but Jim was always so positive and worked so hard it was contagious. They didn't mind the long hours because they were seeing the results, and it was amazing to watch the plant change so quickly. Jim demanded positive attitudes from the entire management team out on the floor. Behind closed doors, he allowed the team to vent and then he would give a little motivational speech that left them willing to run through a door for him. Jim built a team of people from all walks of life that had one goal, which was to succeed.

To say this Agropur plant produces dairy products is not completely accurate. The plant doesn't produce dairy products— the *people* of this Agropur plant, along with a lot of hardworking dairy farmers (and their cows!), produce dairy products. Again, it is the people who generate results. They still made and sold the same product their predecessors did, but they were the right people with the right leader in place. It doesn't matter the widget or service that your company provides. People make you successful.

Jim Mick understood this. His success as a leader was in leading people, not making dairy products. Jim was committed, and he led by example. He was positive and demanded everyone be likewise. He was unselfish with his time and talents.

Although his employees worked hard, Jim provided balance in a number of little ways. He would take his employees to lunch and always pick up the tab. He would demand people take an afternoon off when they needed it. He chartered a bus to take them all to a Detroit Tigers baseball game. He gave them gift cards and told them to take their families to dinner.

Most importantly, Jim Mick made one play of courage. He was willing to make a decision when there was risk involved, knowing if some of the people at Agropur were not willing to jump on board, he would undoubtedly face an uphill battle hiring and training a new team. Yes, Jim was courageous to step up and make changes, but he also demonstrated all the other fundamentals, which helped turn the plant around. Quite simply, he was a *leader*, and he had the courage of his convictions to make them a success.

Looking back, Jim said the hardest thing for people to accept is change, so he made it simple (KISS!) by telling his people "If we keep doing what we are doing then we will keep getting the results we are getting." He focused on meeting with the employees and obtaining their feedback regarding what they saw as obstacles to success. What emerged centered on faulty equipment and lack of operator training. As a result, Jim brought in the equipment vendors necessary to upgrade the machines to operational levels and also gave more detailed training.

"When the employees saw this," Jim said, "it gave our leadership team some credibility that we were doing what we said we would. Due to the line inefficiencies, employees were working seven days a week to complete a five-day schedule. At this point, I put the employees on a four-shift/seven-day operation that guaranteed two days off per week and allowed them the flexibility to plan their lives."

Jim said the next step was to initiate time studies on the lines and document reasons for a stoppage. They needed to know where they were in order to assemble a plan to take them where they needed to be. As they addressed those issues they saw their line efficiencies improve on a weekly basis. This was another opportunity for the leadership group to gain credibility.

"As we continued to improve, our focus shifted to execution and results," Jim said. "If we weren't getting the results we needed, we would course-correct and try a different approach. During this time I also met with our customers and told them what our capability was today and that we would increase our production by ten percent every month until we were servicing our customers at one-hundred percent delivery levels."

Within a year, the plant generated a $22 million swing and profited $11.5 million in that next fiscal year. They went back to the basics and completely changed the attitude within the plant with leading by example, training people properly, and refusing to accept anything less than everyone's best efforts.

Jim trusted his actions each step of the way without a guarantee for results. He had the courage to stick with the plan despite the challenges and adversity. Now that's impacting your success through courage!

* * * * *

TJ Bentley was one member of the management team who survived the transition at Agropur. He describes himself as someone who "will always stand up for what I believe in, even if it is not a popular opinion." TJ talks about the time in 2013 when his company was using one logistics broker for all of its shipping needs. Though TJ was new to this job at the time, he provided an in-depth analysis of what they were doing. In his opinion, they were hemorrhaging money and he wanted to move in a different direction, but he received pushback from corporate because "this is the way we have always done it." (Ever hear that before?)

TJ did not accept that and kept on a-coming! Finally, his boss, who TJ is sure was sick of listening to him talk about this, asked if he was willing to commit to certain cost savings if he could make a change. TJ replied he could knock off $150,000 in their annual spending on freight, even with a projected increase in sales of eighteen percent.

The project was sent to corporate and came back double what he had committed: A cost reduction of $300,000! TJ crunched the numbers again and was positive he could do it, so he accepted their terms. Yes, he admits he was a little scared because everything had to play out just so in order to achieve this goal, and that ultimately, he would be the one to have to answer for it if anything went wrong. That is risky. That is scary. It took courage to stick with it!

After implementing TJ's new logistics plan, they ended the

year with a $664,000 savings in freight costs while increasing sales by thirty-six percent! Having the courage to stand up for what he believed in has saved the company more than $2 million since TJ's plan was implemented.

TJ was relentless in pursuing this goal and had the courage to keep pushing because he knew it would work. As a result he was added to the team in charge of all freight projects for the entire U.S. operation of the company. At thirty-one, he was the youngest person by more than fifteen years on the management team, and he was a leader. By standing up for what he believed in, he put himself in a position to make a difference at Agropur and grow professionally. He is now the head of sales and part-owner of a logistics company and continues to have success.

* * * * *

In today's world, we talk a lot about collaboration and inclusion. I totally agree with both of these concepts and believe I practice them. Perhaps a simpler description of these concepts would be teamwork. Being a part of a team has been a huge part of my life, and I still enjoy being a part of a team today as a consultant, teacher, and author.

However, in order to achieve success, there are times when you alone must make the decision. You can collaborate and gather all the information and opinions you want, but eventually, someone has to decide. Some people have a hard time with this. If you want to be successful, you must have the courage to make decisions.

At some point in every person's career, there is at least one moment when you have to say to yourself, "I'm willing to risk my job in making this decision." Yes, sometimes you have to be willing to go out on that limb in order to be successful. You will make mistakes. Learn from them and try never to repeat them. That's what successful people do. If you know who you are and what you stand for, it's easier to have the courage to risk your job and perhaps your career when needed.

You never know what one act of courage will lead to!

POSITIVITY

"I always like to look at the optimistic side of life, but I am realistic enough to know that life is a complex matter."

– Walt Disney

P atti Phillips of Women Leaders in College Sports is always upbeat and exudes a positivity when you encounter her, either in person, via phone, or even via electronic messaging.

When I asked about her positivity, Patti had this to say: "I am very intentional about being positive. It is a mindset we talk about and practice every day. I work at it!"

Positivity is infectious. Because Patti sets such a positive lead, the staff at Women Leaders in College Sports follow. The office is an open environment and each staff member's energy affects everyone. That's why Patti demands the staff be positive when in the office, and it shows.

Even when Patti receives an email from someone in college athletics criticizing somebody else, she won't reply to it. It drags everybody down when you do. Constructive criticism is one thing; tearing someone down is another.

Women Leaders in College Sports hosts several educational institutes for women who aspire to be leaders in college athletics. They invite already proven leaders in to serve as faculty for these institutes. Patti says she makes sure she and her staff relate positively with those faculty, even down to the most basic email communication. Having been a faculty member for one of these institutes myself, I can verify this is the case. The positivity from Patti and her staff spreads. You cannot help but be upbeat and excited to be a part of their programs.

Recently, the organization lost a $50,000 annual sponsor. Instead of spiraling into the negative about it, Patti's approach was to consider the situation as an opportunity to find a better sponsor. Patti has instilled in her staff that when one door closes, another opens. That's not easy, because you face disappointment, especially when you lose a big sponsor or customer. But dwelling on the negative does no good. Shake it off and look forward to the next opportunity.

In this specific case, Patti made that one play of positivity. She told her team to think differently about how to overcome the loss. Rather than a one-for-one replacement, perhaps here was the chance to increase the number of sponsors. Sure enough, the staff of Women Leaders in College Sports went to work and replaced the $50,000 sponsor with several others that totaled more than $80,000.

That wouldn't have happened if not for the positivity Patti displayed. She didn't let adversity stop her team. That success was because of her positive attitude!

* * * * *

Being positive means more than just happy-go-lucky, smiley face all the time. There are many days you just don't feel that way. But remember, as the leader of your team, however large or small, you set the tone for everyone in the organization. If you have a negative attitude and are down in the dumps, what do you think those you are leading will be? Positive? Probably not. Even if you are not the leader, as a team member, your positivity or negativity will affect everyone around you. Positive people are infectious in successful organizations, like Women Leaders in College Sports.

Mike Guswiler, president of the West Michigan Sports Commission, shares that it is hard to start a new operation, whether it is an entrepreneurial business like Eidex or a nonprofit such as his sports commission. It takes courage, and it also takes a positive attitude.

Mike describes it this way: "Positivity breeds positivity, which breeds success. Negativity takes away so much energy and lessens productivity." Mike talked about bidding on events and tournaments the West Michigan Sports Commission seeks to host. In many cases, the people in charge of the organizations whose bids they are going after will ask for the moon in guarantees. Mike said he and his staff in turn propose only what they are capable of providing, and they are positive about it in their correspondence. They focus on what they *can* do to provide an exemplary experience, not what they can't.

Building a momentum of positivity led Mike's team to land a particularly big fish: the Transplant Games of America. In mid-summer of 2011, Mike heard from the chair of the WMSC board, asking Mike to look into an inquiry he received from a local kidney recipient who had participated for many years in the National Kidney Association's National Transplant Games. The National Kidney Association had conducted these games for a couple decades but decided to end the games in order to apply those budgeted dollars elsewhere.

Mike and his team had just completed a second edition of a multi-sport event in the Meijer State Games of Michigan: Summer Games. Mike invited the state games director to meet with the local kidney recipient and others who had participated in past games. It was from that meeting that Mike and his team decided they would make these games happen. They never thought about whether they *could* do it, but how they *would* do it.

"Our local organizing committee quickly grew with many

others who cared about the competitive enjoyment of the Transplant Games, but even more so about the overall message of The Gift of Life and how these recipients were given another chance at life by donor families and their loved ones," Mike said. "The positivity and the passion for these games created a momentum that carried us through putting on an extremely successful event with many partners . . . all within a relatively short planning window.

"I'm proud to say that we saved these games and that they continue through one of our former board members."

This is a great lesson for all of us. We all have limitations, whether as individuals or as a business. But it's okay to stay within your capabilities. My college coach always used to tell us to "play within your limitations," meaning play to your strengths to help the team and don't try to do things beyond your ability. If you are a shooter, don't try to bull your way to the basket. If you are a rebounder, don't launch three-pointers. That's the same thing Mike Guswiler is saying. Be positive about what you can do and not negative about what you can't.

A positive, can-do attitude made a wonderful event happen successfully. Positivity breeds positivity, which breeds success!

* * * * *

Being positive means several things to me. It means being mature in the face of adversity. It means being thankful for the many wonderful things you have going for you in life. It means being poised when the going gets rough and maintaining emotional control when others around you are losing theirs. It means sometimes just having some fun. It doesn't have to be more complicated than that. If you want to find success, be those things!

Earlier we talked about the turnaround Jim Mick orchestrated at Agropur. Jim sincerely believes the primary reason behind it was simply expressing a positive attitude and being confident it could be accomplished. He admits that some of his employees probably thought he was crazy early on, but after seeing some wins come to fruition, they came onboard fully.

One of the best jobs of staying positive I have ever witnessed comes from Brian Kelly, who was Grand Valley State's head football coach for thirteen years before going on to great success at Central Michigan, Cincinnati, and most recently at Notre Dame.

It was in November of 2001. Grand Valley had just completed the regular season with a 10-0 record and was hosting Bloomsburg University in the first round of the NCAA Division II playoffs. Our best player that year was quarterback Curt Anes. As we marched undefeated during that 2001 season, Curt lit it up.

But in the playoffs against Bloomsburg, adversity hit. We were ahead 28-14 late in the first half and were marching for another score. We had the ball just across midfield and needed only a half-yard for a first down. The idea was to run a quarterback sneak, get a first down to stop the clock, and run another play to try and score again before the half ended. During the sneak, Curt Anes was bent back in the pile and a lot of weight came crashing down on his knee. He tore his ACL, MCL, and PCL. It was obvious his season was over.

I was up in the press box when we heard about the severity of the injury, and I clearly remember thinking our chance at a national championship was in jeopardy. The frustrating thing was that in the storied history of Grand Valley football, we had *never* won an NCAA postseason game. All I could think when Curt went down was we had a monumental challenge ahead of us. But I also knew we had the personnel and the fortitude to meet it.

Somehow, some way, we ended up winning that game to give our school its first playoff win. This is where *being positive* comes in. That team faced adversity. Deep down, everyone knew we just lost the biggest reason we were averaging more than 50 points a game. Brian had to demonstrate to his team we could win two more games and reach the national championship anyway. And that's what he did. Even with such a huge and devastating loss, Coach Kelly and the rest of the team *remained positive.*

Coach Kelly sold his team on the idea that they could still win three more games, only they would have to do it differently than they had done it all year. We went the rest of the playoffs with a wide receiver-turned-QB and ran the ball a lot more. Brian's positive attitude became infectious. In every way, he exhibited a positive attitude. His players were taught the "next man up" concept, which demanded looking forward, not backward. In every conversation with the media, Brian spoke in positive terms about what the team had in front of them to accomplish.

And by changing to a running attack and implementing some option plays we had never used before, we caught our next two opponents off guard and beat both to advance to the national championship game for the first time in Grand Valley's history. Coach Kelly and his players found a way to win by making an adjustment and remaining positive.

* * * * *

Sometimes you're not always sure your idea will work. But as the leader, you have to make those tough decisions, and then be positive in convincing your staff that it will work. You have a chance at success if you do!

I remember my dad almost fifty years ago providing me a teachable moment in this regard during his high school basketball coaching days. My oldest brother Dick was my dad's best player, and one of their opponents deployed a unique defense that devoted two players to guarding Dick wherever he went. While you'd think that wouldn't work, since it left only three players to guard our other four, it was giving them fits. While I was young at the time, I hadn't seen anything like it, and I'm not sure my dad had, either.

He went into halftime not sure what to do. I remember him telling me later, "They were all staring at me with a look that said, 'What should we do?' Even though I wasn't sure of what to do, I *had* to tell them something." What he did during that halftime was devise an offense to counter the double-team defense and sell it to his players, despite never having run it before. It worked; they won the game in overtime.

The lesson here is even if you're not absolutely sure your idea will be effective, you must decide a course of action and be positive in communicating it. Taking risks requires being courageous, and being positive is part of being courageous. If you don't portray a positive attitude, those around you will lose their confidence in you and your abilities, and your idea will almost certainly fail.

Steve Paine of Fab-Lite describes being positive this way: "I have to be the consummate cheerleader who expresses a non-stop passion for Fab-Lite so others will follow." Successful people demonstrate a passion, an enthusiasm, for what they do. Again, this isn't something that can be talked about in a Pollyanna-ish way. Success requires a passion, a deep desire for success for the team. Successful organizations will have a majority of people who are passionate and positive about their work. They have a consistent enthusiasm for the mission. This passion and positivity start at the top. Successful businesses almost always have leaders, like Steve, who have a passion for their work and their people. Successful units of the business have people in them that are passionate and positive. Conversely, unsuccessful organizations are often led by duds and the whole teams tends to perform like duds. Are you passionate and positive, or are you a dud?

Steve admitted that always being the cheerleader can be tiring.

How true. Being positive one-hundred percent of the time takes a great deal of energy, especially in tough situations. Sometimes you have to put on a good front for the rest of the troops even when they are discouraged or tired. That doesn't mean you need to be phony, it just means positivity is demonstrated sometimes by just keeping your poise even when things aren't going well or you're not sure what to do. Again, you have a chance for success if you do!

Here's the point: Life is going to throw you curveballs no matter your career path. You can choose to be negative and complain about things or *you can remain positive* and keep moving forward. I'm not talking about a fake or "Hollywood" version of being positive, either. I'm talking about the kind where you look at the glass as half full; true enthusiasm for what you do. I cannot fathom going through life being negative all the time. There are no statues to honor critics. The less negativity you feed your heart and mind, the more positive you'll become. And the more positive you become, the more success you'll find because you won't have negativity preventing you from being the best you can be.

Brian Kelly was a successful leader for Grand Valley State's football program. He *remained positive* with that 2001 team. Sure, he had to sell his players on believing they could win despite the adversity they faced. But a positive attitude had been ingrained in them. They had a lot to play for, just like you have a lot to live for in your life.

A few days before that first national championship game, I was watching to see if Brian would become uptight, as some coaches do when they finally make it to the big game. After all, neither he nor Grand Valley had ever been in that position before, and it would be the first time the Lakers had played on national television. I was prepared to try and think of something to calm him down, but it was a moot point. As do most great coaches, Brian prepares his teams very well, and the better prepared you are, the more you'll focus positively on the task at hand. It was quickly apparent to me when the Lakers arrived at the site of the national championship game Brian was poised and confident, and his team would be as well.

Brian Kelly used to say when he was trying to teach kids who maybe weren't as talented as others that "Players are like apples—they all have worms; you just have to turn the apple so the shiny side is up!"

People all too often dwell on what they don't have instead of what they do have. We all deal with an imperfect world. Humans have their "worms," as do businesses, schools, and organizations. But you should be thankful for what you have and turn the shiny side up!

It all goes back to *being positive and being thankful for the opportunity.* If you are, chances are you'll have shiny apples along the way.

And as for our 2001 football team? Well, they played great in the national championship game against the University of North Dakota but ended up losing by just three points. We actually took the lead near the end of the game but UND came back with about a minute to go to beat us.

But the loss did not take anything away from that team. The 2001 Grand Valley team was a great success because every one of those kids had experienced Coach John Wooden's definition of success: *Success is a peace of mind, which is the direct result of self-satisfaction in knowing you did your best to become the best you are capable of becoming.* They took a severe blow in the midst of a great run and *stayed positive* to accomplish more than any other team in school history.

This story gets better, too. Most of the 2001 team returned for the 2002 season, and the positive attitude carried over. Curt Anes had surgery, went through rehab, and was back playing again. "Finish what we started" was the team's motto. And that's exactly what they did. But it wasn't without a key moment in which Curt Anes demonstrated the importance of being positive, even in the most stressful situations.

Once again, this team rolled through the competition. They went undefeated in the regular season, won their first three playoff games and advanced to the national championship game against Valdosta State. With the Lakers ahead 24-16 with just over three minutes to play, we had the ball deep in our own territory. Curt Anes couldn't handle the shotgun snap, and Valdosta State recovered the fumble in our end zone for a touchdown and then made the two-point conversion to tie the game.

Often in life, being positive means keeping your composure during difficult challenges and staying calm in order to think more clearly about what needs to be done. Curt kept his composure on the sideline during the ensuing kickoff, reminding our players we still could determine our own fate.

Curt Anes made that one play of positivity, turning adversity into victory by leading the Lakers on a game-winning drive. His TD pass to David Kircus gave the Lakers their first national championship in any sport. And in the spirit of Coach Nichols' favorite saying of "you never know what one play will lead to," Grand Valley has gone on to win twenty-one more national championships (and counting!) in several different sports since then.

* * * * *

You will be defined as a person by how you handle the tough times. When things are good, the bandwagon is full, but what about when potholes appear?

One of my best friends in my profession, college athletics leadership, is Bill Goldring, the now retired, highly successful athletics director at Ashland University, which is a small, private, NCAA Division II school in central Ohio. Under Bill's leadership, the Eagles were always among the top contenders for the Directors' Cup, the national all-sports trophy competition.

Bill and I had a terrific relationship. It is important to have colleagues you can call for feedback and advice, commiserate with when challenges emerge, and sometimes just share a laugh or two. Bill was and still is that person for me. We would take turns talking about whatever had gone wrong in our programs, and in the end, Bill would say something like, "It's just sports for crying out loud," and we'd have a laugh and all was good. I always left any conversation with Bill with a positive attitude and a smile.

Deb Bailey was director of global corporate relations for Steelcase, one of the world's largest manufacturers of office furniture. She has never been the CEO but has always been in middle leadership. She describes herself as a "perpetual junior" and believes being successful at the middle leadership level means you must "know who you are," or be comfortable in your skin. You don't have to be the CEO to find success.

Remaining positive often requires keeping things in perspective. Similar to Bill Goldring's philosophy, Deb would tell her employees, "It's just office furniture." We all tend to take ourselves too seriously. My good friend and lawyer from Toledo, Mike Spiros, put it best by saying we should take our jobs seriously but not take ourselves seriously.

But what about when a crisis hits?

Deb found herself placed on a team of four people in January of 2001 charged with developing a process for laying off 10,000 employees. They weren't being asked to make the decisions, just to figure out a way to execute a plan that would have the least amount of impact on the employees losing their jobs and the company as a whole. There's nothing positive about that. And in all reality, there's not much that can be described as successful about that, either. People should always be your most important resource, and every possible fix should be explored before going to layoffs. However, Steelcase upper-level leadership made the decision: The company needed to change what it was doing in order to move forward in the marketplace.

That doesn't mean you can't have a positive attitude when attacking a crisis like this.

"We prepared materials/scripts for every manager to talk to their people being laid off individually, so every laid-off employee was met with individually with their manager and their HR person for support," Deb said. "We also prepared scripts for every manager to have meetings with their teams after each round of layoffs to share feelings/thoughts and impact. All salaried people received outplacement support and hourly people also had access to resources for unemployment and reemployment possibilities. We created guiding principles which put 'treating the affected employee with respect and dignity' first in the entire process and in all that we designed and did."

The team's plan called for Steelcase to go to great lengths protecting the health and safety of every individual. Those efforts cost Steelcase a ton of money, but Deb accurately pointed out not doing so would have cost a lot more in lawsuits and lost productivity. Deb and her team made that one play of positivity.

"People were at the center of everything and we did not allow ourselves to become negative or lazy at any point in the process," Deb said.

The remaining employees observed the process and had to decide if they could continue to trust leadership to do the right thing. Although this was among the most challenging professional situations Deb had ever faced, she said she at least gained some sense of satisfaction that no lawsuits were filed and that the rest of the employees committed to a brighter future. Current employee surveys reinforce Steelcase's reputation as a great place to work. Total employment at the company is also increasing, from under 6,000 total company employees during the mid-2000s, to 12,000 currently, according to their website.

Deb's positive attitude about life is demonstrated in her own personal health as well. She has faced four bouts of cancer and will not let it defeat her! When discussing this with Deb she always has a smile on her face while sharing her battles with cancer and will often throw some humor into the conversation (and we all know there is nothing humorous about this disease). But it is her positive approach to life that is evident when you are around her. Isn't that the kind of person you want to work with? Isn't that the type of person you want to be?

The whole idea of being positive is critical in achieving any kind of success, whether it's in athletics, education, business, or life. It's easy to be dragged down by adversity, but you do your best when you *remain positive* and *be thankful* for your opportunities. No one was thankful at the time GVSU fumbled in the end zone, but I truly believe that adversity brought out the best in our team. Instead of complaining, they remained *positive* and found a way to win anyway.

You never know what demonstrating poise and emotional control will lead to. You never know what one expression of maturity will lead to. And you never know what having a positive attitude will lead to. Life isn't a fairy tale, and there are no guarantees to anything, but if you can *be positive and thankful for the opportunities and the people around you*, regardless of the situation, you have a better chance at achieving John Wooden's "peace of mind," which is a direct result of self-satisfaction in knowing you did your best to become the best you are capable of becoming.

You never know what one play of positivity will lead to!

Unselfishness

We have a good chance of getting a smile from someone if we first offer that person a smile. To receive a letter, we first need to send a letter. If we expect a unique blessing, spiritual etiquette would say we must first offer a prayer. We might complain about our situation and feel neglected both by God and others because we have not received something, yet the first question is to ask how much we have given.

Generosity is one of those talents and lights not to be hidden under a basket. Others need to see and know about our abilities and good works, for that causes them to consider how they can do better. Selfishness is difficult to overcome, but examples of unselfish giving by others can be inspiring to those who have become self-centered. If we are generous with our time, money and mercy, we can inspire and enlighten others.

What we give, we get in return; that applies both to curses and blessings.

– Anonymous

One of the most unselfish student-athletes in the history of Grand Valley State's volleyball program was a young lady by the name of Clair Ruhenkamp. People everywhere in all walks of life and of all ages could learn a lesson from this collegiate student-athlete. Yes, we can learn from twenty-two-year-olds!

Clair was the starting setter from day one of her freshman year. She started every match and performed well. She started every match her sophomore year as well. Our team compiled decent win-loss records, but our coaches were concerned Clair wasn't progressing as well as they would have liked. So they recruited a junior college All-American setter, Kaitlyn Wolters, to join the team. Clair now had competition.

After two weeks of nonconference play at the start of Clair's junior year, it was apparent she was no longer the first-string setter on the team; she would become the backup to Kaitlyn.

Okay, so here's a classic case of personal challenge and overcoming adversity. All of us have likely been in a similar situation at some point in our lives—you're accustomed to serving in one role and then are asked (perhaps told) to shift into another that is clearly a demotion (at least in your eyes). How do you handle it? How do you help others handle these kinds of situations?

Instead of becoming a problem on the team, Clair re-emerged with an unselfishness young people (or adults for that matter) rarely display and became one of the best leaders ever in our program. She made that one play of unselfishness.

During her exit interview after her senior year, Clair told the story from her point of view. She described how after she was told she would no longer be the starter, she had a pity party for herself and called her mom that night to tell her what was happening. Her mom (thank you, Mrs. Ruhenkamp, for being a wonderful example as a parent) basically explained to her she had two directions she could go. She could choose a selfish path and make this be all about her, or she could selflessly figure out how else she could contribute meaningfully to the team. Thankfully for GVSU Volleyball, Clair chose the latter.

As the athletics director and being aware of the situation, I strolled down to practice about a week after Clair was demoted and asked Coach Deanne Scanlon how she was handling it. Deanne said she had a great attitude and was being very mature about it. Our team had a good year and went to the NCAA tournament.

During the middle of the following season, Clair's senior year and her second year as a backup setter, I checked in with Deanne again about Clair. Our team was having an outstanding year, and Clair was a big reason why. Deanne flat out said Clair was one of the most impactful players we'd ever had. She explained Clair had taken it upon herself to become an active voice on the second team, and her leadership during practice was so phenomenal it helped push the first team to be that much better. We advanced all the way to the national semifinals that year and the most impactful player on the team was our backup setter!

In an article after her career was over, Clair provided the following quote all leaders can learn from: *"You can't control your circumstances, but you can control your attitude."*

And she's right, you can't always control everything. Clair Ruhenkamp chose to be unselfish under tough circumstances and made an impact on the second unit, thus allowing the entire team to achieve success. She is now an elementary school teacher (again, great leaders teach!) in Ohio and is passing on her positive and unselfish attitude to hundreds of children each year.

"The best part of my job is applying my ability to positively impact our youth," Clair told me recently. "Every day I watch students overcome challenges inside and outside of the classroom. And every year I am able to help students who can't read or who may dislike reading become reading *machines*. I am also able to help teach life skills and lessons to students with tough home lives in hopes it will carry on with them afterward. I experience the opportunity to help them reach goals and grow as individuals, which is more rewarding than any medal or prize I've ever won."

In addition to her teaching, Clair has also coached eighth-grade volleyball and is now coaching a junior varsity team. Her unselfish nature emerges as she describes how her volleyball career has shaped her as a coach: "I love sharing my knowledge of the game and sharing my own personal experiences while on the court and being on the sidelines to help players grow. I can honestly say my experience with volleyball at Grand Valley State has helped me to relate to all of my players and students. I am able to have a strong connection to the student who excels in the classroom or the player who excels on the court, while also understanding the student or player who puts all of the work in and doesn't get the results they want."

Clair earned a master's degree in education administration from the University of Dayton with a 3.9 GPA. She hopes to be a principal in the future. She makes an impact like many that teach and coach: Clair is driven by her desire to help others. She knows if she succeeds in helping her students and her players, they will find success and so will she. Her unselfish character displayed as a college student-athlete is now being used to help young people. That is the kind of leader I want working with today's youth!

* * * * *

Jeff Dock was a quarterback on the two Grand Valley State football teams I talked about in the last chapter. Jeff's story is similar to Clair Ruhenkamp's, but there's a twist. Clair began her college career as a starter and became a backup, while Jeff spent all but two games of his entire career on the second unit.

Jeff was good enough to start and excel on most other teams in our league, but his timing was unfortunate at Grand Valley. He entered as the backup to Curt Anes, who led our program to its first national championship, and then after Curt graduated, Jeff served as the backup to the late Cullen Finnerty, who led us to national championships in 2003, 2005, and 2006 and has the most wins as a QB in the history of NCAA football, regardless of division.

Jeff could have transferred to another school, but he wanted to pursue his education at Grand Valley and not transfer just to play football. He sacrificed his chance for more playing time elsewhere by remaining at GVSU and making an impact on four national championship teams.

Unselfishness involves sacrifice. Sacrifice is defined as *"surrendering something prized or desirable for the sake of something considered as having a higher or more pressing claim."*

The bottom line is Jeff spent five years in our program and started only two games. But like many backup QBs, he served as the holder on all of our field goals and extra points. Although it's not as glamorous as being the starting QB, being the holder is a pretty important job in football. You only notice them when they fumble a snap and screw things up. That never happened with Jeff. He sacrificed being a quarterback and accepted a smaller role on the field. The team benefitted from his unselfish attitude. Many people are in Jeff's shoes. They play unsung roles in their organization, yet their impact on their unit or division is just as vital to the team's success as the CEO.

Jeff was a real luxury for our coaches because they knew if anything ever happened to either starting QB, they were confident Jeff could lead our team. Even though Jeff was a backup player for almost his entire career, there are many of us, myself included, who consider him one of the most significant players we ever had.

Here's why.

If you recall the story I told you of our 2001 Grand Valley football team and the challenge they faced when Curt Anes was injured, you will remember that we won our next two games and made it to the national championship game. In that playoff run we had to convert to being a running team after Curt was hurt. The receiver-turned-quarterback we used to replace Curt couldn't throw deep balls very well. His ability to run the option had worked well, but by the time we advanced to the national championship game, our opponent, the University of North Dakota, had figured that out. They were preparing to position most of their defensive players up close to the line of scrimmage to stop the run and dare us to throw deep. Coach Brian Kelly was faced with a dilemma.

We did have one quarterback in the program who had a strong enough arm to throw it deep and keep North Dakota's defense honest. That was Jeff Dock. But Jeff was in his first year in the program and was being redshirted, meaning he couldn't play in the games or he'd use up a season of eligibility. Recently, the NCAA rule changed, and it now allows players to participate in up to four games before designating a year as a red-shirt season. At that time, though, NCAA rules didn't even allow you to play for one minute or even one play or you lost a season of eligibility.

On Monday morning the week of the championship game, Coach Kelly entered my office and said he was thinking of burning Jeff's redshirt year and playing him in the championship game. That meant Jeff's entire redshirt season could be used on a series or perhaps one play, just so we could try and throw deep to keep North Dakota's defense honest.

Coach Kelly said he had already talked to Jeff's dad, a highly successful high school coach who understood the situation, and thought Jeff would do what's best for the team. That's exactly what Jeff Dock did. He told Coach Kelly if it was best for the team, then let's go ahead and burn his redshirt year.

Now that is being unselfish! That is sacrificing! (i.e., "surrendering something prized or desirable for the sake of something considered as having a higher or more pressing claim.")

The happy ending here is while we lost the game, we did not end up using Jeff to keep the defense honest. But the point is if he had been needed, Jeff was committed to helping the team. That gave Coach Kelly the confidence he needed heading into the week of preparations for that game. Jeff was willing to put one of his four seasons of eligibility on the line. That's the unselfishness I'm talking about that can impact your success, the kind we need more of in this world.

Our coaches will tell you they knew everything was okay in the locker room because they had Jeff in there making sure everyone kept the team above self. You think it has an impact on young men when someone who never gets the chance to be a starter has the best attitude on the team? You bet it does.

Jeff Dock was looking out for the greater good of our

program. Why? He was *being unselfish.* He cared about the team ahead of his own interests. It wasn't easy. He certainly became discouraged at times and was frustrated by not getting his shot to be our starting quarterback. But he didn't let that get in the way of making an impact. He made that one play of unselfishness.

* * * * *

Ask yourself this question: "Why do I do what I do?" I believe to have success you have to do what you do for a *greater cause than your own.* If the answer to that question is "to make money," I believe you will not have a fulfilling career. If the answer to that question is "to win games" or "to be in the hall of fame" or "to win awards," I believe you will not have a fulfilling career. In order to meet John Wooden's definition of success, you must *be unselfish* in your chosen career.

My first job after college was as a math teacher, assistant boys basketball coach, and head boys tennis coach at Springfield High School, just outside of Toledo. It was a great year for me. Sometimes it was very difficult because it was my first year of teaching, which I presume is the toughest for most teachers. But I learned a great deal during that year and will always appreciate the principal at the time, Jake Prentiss, for hiring me, and Pat Cunningham, the head basketball coach, for mentoring me about teaching and coaching at a suburban high school.

I have been fortunate in my life to have had many wonderful mentors who really cared about me and cared about what was best for me even though it may have caused them some extra work. That's *being unselfish.*

Pat Cunningham was one of those mentors. He not only taught me a lot in the one year we spent together, but he knew my ambition was to return to college athletics. In the summer after my first year at Springfield, Bob Nichols, my head coach at Toledo, called and offered me the chance to come back and be one of his assistant coaches. This presented a difficult decision for me, as I was slated to be the head boys' varsity coach at Springfield in the coming year, since Pat had retired as coach and had moved up to be the athletics director. Pat had basically groomed me to take his place as the head coach. But when the opportunity to return to college athletics at the age of twenty-four presented itself, both Pat and Jake Prentiss told me they understood and that I had to take it. I will always appreciate their unselfishness. They cared about me more than their own interests. I've since tried my best to do the same for others.

My wife Terry and I were married on July 24, 1982. When we returned from our honeymoon, I began my job as an assistant men's basketball coach at Toledo. I remember thinking as I got out of my car and walked into the arena that first day, "Okay, it's time to go to work. Go help those kids have the same experience you had."

And that's what I have tried to do. That was the "why" for being in college athletics. Providing the best programs possible for the student-athletes who competed in them was the success I was trying to achieve. Sure I was competitive, but the "why" wasn't about wins and titles, making money and moving up the ladder. College athletics should be about putting the student-athletes' experiences above your own.

And that should be the job of any leader. It's simple: If leaders help their staffs be successful, they'll be successful.

Another mentor to me early on was someone I have referred to earlier in the book, John Savage. I had numerous conversations with John during the early years of my career, and I found him to be genuinely unselfish. Of all of the things I remember from him, what stuck with me most was when he simply said, "Everybody needs a little help along the way."

Yes, we all have to hold our own, and we all have to make a commitment to being successful, but nobody lives on an island. Most people who think others ought to "pick themselves up by the bootstraps" have had the good fortune of being helped by others. They just don't appreciate others who have helped them along the way. *Being unselfish* means going out of your way to help others, as well as appreciating others who go out of their way to help you.

*   *   *   *   *

Grand Rapids, Michigan, in my opinion, is one of the finest mid-sized cities in the country. Among what makes Grand Rapids great is the level of philanthropy that exists in West Michigan. Downtown Grand Rapids is vibrant. Occupancy rates of businesses and housing are at their highest levels ever, unlike most Midwest Rust Belt cities. The wealthy among our community lead the way. They may have ample resources, but they genuinely care about their community and the people in it, and they give back in ways that don't call attention to themselves. I know. I've seen how hard some of them work on causes that do nothing for them personally. They do it because they are simply *being unselfish*. They are doing it for the greater good.

It all started in April of 1991 with the Grand Vision Committee. At that time, Grand Rapids was similar to many Midwest cities with very little commercial and entertainment activity downtown. It was a ghost town on the weekends, and crime was high.

Rich DeVos, one of the founders of Amway, was a business leader in the community. He assembled more than fifty community leaders and volunteers from the business, labor, civic, academic, and sports sectors to explore the possibility of building an arena and expanding and renovating local convention facilities. In 1992 the name was officially changed to Grand Action and two local banking leaders, John Canepa and David Frey, joined DeVos as co-chairs. As stated on the Grand Action website:

> *Grand Action is a not-for-profit organization comprised of more than 250 individuals from throughout the community. Its primary objectives have been to identify downtown building and revitalization projects, to galvanize public opinion and support for these projects, and to design and implement funding strategies for each project, including securing enough private*

sector support to guarantee funding from existing public funds.

In other words, philanthropy is more than just donating dollars. Read the excerpt above once again. Unselfish leaders give *more* than money for the common good. Money solves some problems but not all. Adding unselfish leadership is what makes a city successful. *People* do that, not money.

Grand Action was formed in 1991. It took time and commitment, but Grand Rapids has thrived as a city ever since. Private investments of $125 million have triggered more than $420 million in downtown capital investments, according to a report from the Philanthropic Collaborative and the Council for Michigan Foundations. Crime rates have dropped significantly in the past ten years. And in February of 2017, Grand Rapids was ranked in the top 20 best cities to live, according to *U.S. News and World Report.*

* * * * *

This chapter started with the story of Clair Ruhenkamp. Following Clair's senior year, I received a call from the National Association of Collegiate Directors of Athletics (NACDA). One of NACDA's primary corporate donors was sponsoring a float in the Rose Bowl Parade, and they wanted to populate the float with athletes from different sports. They needed a volleyball player and NACDA wanted to know if I had one in mind. It was a no-brainer. The young lady who was one of the most unselfish, impactful players ever at Grand Valley State deserved to ride on that float. Clair Ruhenkamp enjoyed a wonderful experience participating in the Rose Bowl Parade!

Most of us in life are not at the top of our profession. We may never be the starting setter or starting quarterback in our organizations, but don't let that stop you from *being unselfish.* You will be surprised at how much better you will feel about yourself, your profession, and your professional life when you put others ahead of yourself. Clair Ruhenkamp had a choice to make when she was designated the backup setter. She chose to be the best she could be for the second unit on our team. She sacrificed her chance to transfer and start at another school, and wound up making a significant impact on our team's success.

What choice will you make when confronted with adversity as Clair was? Will you sacrifice? Will you *"surrender something prized or desirable for the sake of something considered as having a higher or more pressing claim?"*

You never know what one play of unselfishness will lead to!

COMMITMENT

"Success is peace of mind, which is a direct result of self-satisfaction in knowing you did your best to become the best you are capable of becoming."

– John Wooden

I n *Anchor Up: Competitive Greatness the Grand Valley Way*, I shared a story about commitment that involved one of our tennis players turning a seemingly meaningless match into a pivotal moment for our entire athletics department.

It was the spring of 1999, three years after I was hired as the director of athletics at Grand Valley State. Before I arrived, Grand Valley had struggled to win a conference championship in any sport, but by 1999 our athletics program had the opportunity to do something that hadn't been done at the school in twenty years, which was to win the Presidents' Cup, the all-sports trophy awarded to the Great Lakes Intercollegiate Athletic Conference (GLIAC) school whose programs have been the most successful during that year.

It all came down to the GLIAC men's tennis championship. Our team was playing for third place, which may not seem like a big deal, but I was one of just a couple people who knew what was at stake. If we could finish third in men's tennis, we would clinch the Presidents' Cup.

For three years as the new athletics director, I had created the vision of being an all-around, highly competitive athletics program. Grand Valley State had a winning tradition in football, but we didn't have a great deal of overall success in our athletics program, and I was committed to changing our underachieving ways. With this match, we had a chance to validate our dream of being a successful broad-based intercollegiate athletics program. (People have asked me why, if winning the Presidents' Cup was a stated goal, would I not share this with everyone. Well, I did not want to add any pressure to the team. Plus there is that karma thing in athletics you know—by telling everyone we would jinx ourselves!)

And at that moment it was all up to a kid named Chris Penzien. The other players had finished their matches and the overall match was tied at four wins apiece. Chris's match was all that was left to break the tie. He didn't know it had anything to do with the Presidents' Cup. Nobody there did. Quite simply, this match seemingly had little meaning. It was for third place; it wasn't televised; there would be no trophies awarded; and as I recall, I was the only spectator!

Chris Penzien was about five foot nine and weighed a buck-thirty soaking wet. He was not intimidating by any means, but for those of you who play tennis, he was the kind of player who drove his opponent nuts. Chris would track down every ball hit his way and send it back. He ran down everything! He used his quickness to succeed because he certainly wasn't going to overpower anyone. Simply put, he out-hustled his opponents by keeping the ball in play and making them make the mistakes.

Chris Penzien had that fundamental of commitment. Many people work hard and put a lot of hours into what they do, but to achieve real success, there must be a *commitment* to the cause. You must believe in the vision and be dedicated to what your group or organization is trying to achieve. Without that, you won't reach your full potential, nor will your organization. It doesn't matter whether it is in your work, your family life, your school experience, your spiritual life, your volunteer efforts—whatever it may be—hard work must be backed by a commitment to achieve sustained success.

There are several definitions of the word "commit," but the one that applies to successful leadership is from Webster's: *"the state or an instance of being obligated or emotionally impelled—a commitment to a cause."* Chris Penzien was committed to giving his very best effort when it seemingly didn't matter to anyone. There were no spectators at that match other than me. No pep band, no cheerleaders, and no TV cameras. Successful people always feel an obligation to give their best and to be emotionally invested even when no one else seems to care or is paying attention. Many often express they just don't think their boss cares. So what? Be committed anyway. Eventually your commitment will impact those around you and good things will happen!

Here is another critical fact about the Chris Penzien match: It was finals week at Grand Valley, and upon the conclusion of this tournament, all of the players were going home for the summer. In a college tennis match under normal circumstances, if the score is tied at 4-4 all of the players from each team will gather around the court and cheer for their one remaining player on every point. In this case, though, all of the other players were ready to go home. They were all laying around on the side courts chatting and not paying particular attention to Chris' match. When the match went to a third set, you could almost hear the groans. Players from both teams just wanted it to end. It was a consolation match for crying out loud. It didn't matter.

Thank goodness for Grand Valley State athletics it mattered to one guy . . . Chris Penzien!

I remember when Chris finished out the match and won the final point. He gave a little hop and pumped his fist. It was important to him that he was committed to giving his best even when no one else cared. When the match was over I congratulated Chris. Our team had no idea they had just won the Presidents' Cup for Grand Valley.

We won a lot of championships at Grand Valley State in the succeeding years, but I'm not sure I have ever been as proud of one individual as I was of Chris that day. Chris didn't know his match would determine whether Grand Valley would win its first Presidents' Cup in twenty years, but he was still committed to winning, even though it was a consolation match in a conference tournament.

When I got in my car I called Tim Nott, our associate athletics director for media relations, who had informed me we had a chance to win the Presidents' Cup with a third-place finish. I told him we beat Michigan Tech and finished third and asked him if he was sure we won the Cup. He assured me we did and I'll never forget what I said next: "I want you to know, Chris Penzien just played his guts out to win that match for us!" I said it with emotion in my voice then and I still get emotional when I think about it now. When I think of commitment, I think of a skinny Division II tennis player playing his guts out when nobody was watching and nobody cared!

After graduating from Grand Valley, Chris taught chemistry (successful leaders teach!) for several years before moving into the lab as a bench chemist at Perrigo, an American international manufacturer of private label over-the-counter pharmaceuticals. He held positions of increasing responsibility and eventually was promoted to Quality Assurance Senior Manager.

When I asked Chris to reflect on that tennis match in April of 1999, he told me he has always been a competitive person, and that no matter what he does, he tries to be the best at it. Tennis provided Chris an outlet to focus that determination in college. He worked harder than almost anyone because he wanted it the most. Every time he stepped on the court, he wanted to win for himself, for his team, and for his school.

"The match at the conference tournament that year was no different," Chris said. "I had lost to my opponent earlier that season in three sets, and I didn't want that to happen again. Also, third place in the conference might not seem like a big deal in and of itself, but for me it was.

"I knew the match was on my racket, as I saw our number five singles player losing his final set, so I knew the score was 4-4. I played hard. I knew my opponent was feeling the pressure, too. I came to the net more than I normally would just to throw him off—I was normally a total baseline player. I remember match point distinctly. I came to the net and he tossed a lob over my backhand side. I hit a backhand overhead winner and yelled 'Come on!' so loud that I'm guessing everyone in the club heard me."

At the time Chris said he had no idea that match was anything more than securing us third place. But everything he had already learned from his years on the tennis court taught him you fight for every point and try to be the best you can, no matter the circumstance.

"Win or lose, I wanted to hold my head up high when I walked off the court. That mentality has served me well in my career and personal life as well," Chris said. "When I moved into the lab as an entry-level chemist, I worked hard. I wanted to be the best—not because I thought it would help me receive a promotion or a raise, but because if something is worth doing, it's worth doing well.

"That competitive spirit has not died out with age. While I may have learned to control myself enough to be a bit more fun to play board games with, I still try to put my all in everything I do. Looking back, playing for Grand Valley is one of the things I'm most proud of in my life, and unknowingly leaving a small legacy behind by helping us win the Presidents' Cup is something I won't ever forget."

That's a man who understands commitment!

You never know what being committed will do for you and your organization. Maybe it's simply grinding through another workday to keep the organization moving forward in the marketplace. Maybe it's taking a little extra time with the new student or hire. Maybe it's going out of your way to praise an employee that motivates them to do something extraordinary. Or maybe it's sucking it up and digging deep in a seemingly meaningless tennis match that allows your school to win the all-sports trophy for the first time in twenty years. All it takes is the ability to get up every morning and give your best effort that day. You can do that.

Grand Valley has gone on to win twenty-one (and counting) consecutive Presidents' Cups and thirteen Directors' Cups, the *national* all-sports trophy for NCAA Division II. Would that have happened if Chris Penzien hadn't made that one play of commitment in April of 1999? All I know is that from then on, everyone in our athletics department knew we could do this. Not only that, once we tasted success, you could sense a feeling of "we aren't giving this up." Our commitment level rose even higher. We were committed to the hard work of recruiting, coaching, and helping young kids reach their potential.

Achieving success in any profession is hard work, and you can't get there without *commitment.* Thankfully, we had a fine example in one young man who showed us what can be accomplished because of one great effort . . . a *commitment* to be at his best whether it mattered or not.

* * * * *

Think back to John Wooden's definition of success at the beginning of this chapter. He called it the peace of mind that comes from the self-satisfaction in knowing you did your best to become the best you are capable of becoming. Think about the times you had that wonderful feeling of genuine satisfaction because you knew you "did your best," just as your parents, teachers, coaches, employers, clergy, and so on had encouraged you to do your whole life.

Attaining the success Wooden defines takes *commitment,* the kind Chris Penzien demonstrated throughout his career, and in particular on that Saturday afternoon in April of 1999. It is essential that you are committed to being the best you can be if you want those around you to do likewise.

I once heard Lou Holtz, the hall of fame college football coach and analyst for televised games, talk about why he failed as a coach in professional football. He was successful at several stops at the college level and was lured to take on the head coaching job with the NFL's New York Jets. Holtz took the job rationalizing that if it didn't work out, he would come back to college coaching. That is exactly what happened. By making a half-hearted commitment, Holtz doomed himself to failure. That's a great lesson for everyone.

My first job was in the sixth grade. I was twelve years old. Every Saturday I had to get up early instead of sleeping in and work from 8 a.m. to noon at the Rychener Seed Company in Pettisville, Ohio. One of my jobs was to sweep the basement. Imagine the basement of a seed company—dirty, dank, dark, and once in a while I would see something with a long tail scurrying about along the wall.

While nobody, particularly my boss, Joe Rychener, was ever going to inspect how well I cleaned the corners with that broom, I was committed to answering to a higher authority as only God and I would know if I did the job well or not.

My mother had instilled in me and my brothers at a young age that if we were going to do a job—any job—do it right. My mother even evaluated how straight my rows were when I mowed the lawn, and whether I cut all of the grass on the turns. (It was in my best interests to understand what making a commitment was all about!)

As time went on, Joe gave me greater responsibilities than just sweeping. I would bag the seed into fifty-pound bags and stack them up on a pallet. I can't say I was an expert at creating straight stacks, but only a few fell off and split open. Regardless of how good I was as a seed bagger (and Joe probably wouldn't classify me as adept), I did learn something about working and making a commitment to show up on time and do the best job I could.

* * * * *

Most of us are in some position of leadership in our lives. Many of us are parents, which is one of the toughest leadership positions there is. In the workplace, chances are you're in some sort of leadership role, whether it's obvious or not. You might not be the president or CEO, but you're probably in charge of supervising someone, teaching someone, or helping a group achieve a desired outcome. Almost all of us are in middle leadership positions. Almost all of us have someone we report to and have people reporting to us. Regardless of your leadership role, you need that fundamental of commitment.

If you accept a position of leadership at work, be committed to it. If you become a parent, be committed to it. If you choose to volunteer in your community, be committed to it. Success in leadership starts with *commitment!*

I was the AD at Grand Valley State for twenty years and enjoyed great success by any measure during this time. As I look back, I realize there were many reasons for our success. We had a talented staff that worked hard and knew their stuff, and they cared about kids. We were fortunate to be part of a great school that helped us attract talented and hard-working student-athletes, which is essential for success in college athletics.

Having said all of that, though, I believe the single biggest reason we had success is these people were *committed* to the Grand Valley State athletics program. We had stability on our staff, which also is a critical ingredient for success. Think about the best teams you've been associated with or know about. I bet most of them have stability in leadership. They have people who are committed to that school or organization. That holds true for any endeavor. You must have people who are committed to your mission.

Grand Valley is a good example. If you don't know much about the NCAA and its three-division structure, you might think the NCAA is composed only of the big schools like Ohio State, Texas, and Alabama, since they're who you see regularly on TV during football and basketball season. But Grand Valley is among about 300 NCAA colleges and universities that are members of Division II. Division II differs from Division I in that student-athletes who choose to participate in sports aren't expected to do so as a full-time endeavor. They may be just as competitive (and in some cases just as talented) as their Division I counterparts, but the Division II experience lets them live a more balanced college life.

Many people assume people in Division II athletics are constantly aspiring to "go to the next level," which is Division I. While for some that is indeed the case, for others—like me— it's about realizing where you can make the most meaningful contribution and be committed to achieving success at that level.

I came to Grand Valley from Toledo, which is a Division I school. Throughout my first ten years at GVSU, people would always ask me, "Are you going to move on to become an AD in Division I?" I understood why people asked the question, but that's not what I wanted in my career. In fact I would argue it's not what most people want in their career. Remember Wooden's definition of success? I was thirty-eight years old and I had been the associate AD at my alma mater for eight years. I wanted to become an AD at a school where we could be successful and in a place where my wife and I could raise our family.

I had grown up in Pettisville, Ohio, and attended kindergarten through my senior year of high school in the same school. Back then, Pettisville was a town of about 400 people (it probably has 450 now, it's really growing!). I graduated with a class of fifty-two. I saw my father have a fantastic teaching and coaching career at this small school in a terrific town to raise a family. We had deep roots in that community.

Although I've been gone from "P-Ville" for a long time, whenever I am asked where I'm from, I still say Pettisville, Ohio. That's what I wanted for me and my family. That's who I was. I didn't want to be a nomad in college athletics and wander from school to school to try to "make it to the top." All I wanted was to be a successful athletics director at a good school in a location where we would enjoy raising our family.

During the interview at Grand Valley State, I knew we had found that place. And once I had convinced myself of that, the next goal was for me to help Grand Valley athletics be the best it could possibly be. I was *committed* to that goal. I wasn't committed to being at Grand Valley for a few years and then moving on. I was committed to making Grand Valley the pinnacle of success.

And where did it lead? In addition to the professional success at Grand Valley, I was also able to make a meaningful contribution to my community. We became entrenched in the Parish of the Holy Spirit, our church. I am an usher, served on our school Education Foundation board for three terms, and co-chaired our parish's capital campaign. I became a board member of the West Michigan Sports Commission since its inception in 2006 and served four three-year terms. I belonged to Grand Rapids Downtown Rotary for twenty years, serving on the program committee. I was able to serve on several governance committees with the NCAA and NACDA, the professional association of athletics directors. I would never have had these wonderful opportunities to grow and contribute professionally and personally if I had jumped from job to job.

Part of that was knowing commitment starts at the top, but it also involved long-term thinking. If I was going to ask everyone else in our programs to be committed, I had to be committed as well. If I wanted my staff to plan and think long-term, I had to as well. And if I wanted to convince my bosses to think long-term, I had to demonstrate to them that I was in it for the long haul. Think about that wherever you now work and for whomever you have worked. Those leaders making decisions only to "make a splash" in the near term for selfish reasons could have had stamped on their foreheads "I need to build my résumé to make me look good so I can move on to the next job."

Contrast that with those leaders who were planning way down the road and had a vision for what the organization could become and outlined all of the details and hard work that needed to take place. Those leaders are unselfish and always thinking of the greater good. It is much easier to follow those kinds of leaders. If you can't buy in and be totally committed to your workplace or organization, then it might be time to look at doing something else. Truly successful individuals and organizations are committed to their cause. Commitment breeds stability, which breeds success.

* * * * *

Parenting is probably the most important leadership role one can play, and it might be the most challenging leadership role there is because you only have one chance to get it right. Being a single parent is without a doubt more challenging. There is no way you can succeed in parenting without being committed.

Sandra Jennings, a single parent of two children, exemplifies this. This story can perhaps apply to numerous situations in your life, whether you are a parent or not. It is a story of making a tough decision and sticking with it.

Commitment was engrained in Sandra when she was just a kid. "I grew up with a mother who worked in a factory all her life, with a step-father who was a twenty-four-hour on-call mortician, and a father who served forty-four years of perfect attendance at General Motors," Sandra said. "That was the mentality I was raised to emulate."

But on one day in 1993 perfect attendance at work didn't matter. Her daughter, Myia, suffered from what their family believes was an undiagnosed mental illness. When Myia was twelve and entering middle school, her progress took a downward turn and things became difficult for her. "Her undiscerning spirit began to fail her, and she started hanging out with the wrong crowd. I was worrying constantly, and it began to take a toll on my workplace performance. Needless to say, when her grades slipped my worrying turned to panic. And the workplace became more and more intolerant of me. I had always felt that they had had enough of me being distracted with family traumas . . . always on the phone with this problem or that problem, being called to the principal's office repeatedly."

Eventually, after a weekend where Myia acted out on a new level, Sandra sat her daughter down. "I threatened that if I had to be called to the school one more time, then she was going to live with her father in California. The man who had not shown up in her life to any degree of regularity. The man who never paid child support. The man who rarely sent birthday cards.

"The thought alone of me sending her there scared me to

tears. He was remarried to a lady who had two children of her own, and together they had a young son. But I knew if Myia continued down the path she was headed, it was not going to end well for her."

Well, Myia called Sandra's bluff later that week. She had skipped school on a Thursday and didn't return until late in the evening. Sandra told her to pack her bags.

"The whole family cried," she said. "She and her brother embraced like it was the last time they would see each other. I was separating them, and it broke my heart. But I knew if I didn't take drastic measures, it might mean losing Myia to some God-awful element where she might not return in one piece."

Company policy at Sandra's place of work mandated employees provide notice before taking a day off. Knowing this, she repeatedly called her boss and left messages with his wife. He refused to take her call. Sandra had to make a decision: Be committed to helping her troubled daughter or go to work for a boss who didn't respect her family issues. For Sandra, the choice was easy. She took the day off to be with her daughter and see her off to California, and returned to work the following Monday.

"I went to work and arrived earlier than everyone else, just like normal. When I got to my desk there was a typed memo that read, 'Family emergency notwithstanding, your request for vacation is denied.' I found myself staring at that note in disbelief. It wasn't the loss of wages for those eight hours. It was the lack of empathy for what was the most traumatic experience in my young life. I began to relive every minute of that painful weekend. I started crying uncontrollably. Then I got mad. So I went home and sat there angry . . . for about five minutes. Then I typed my resignation letter. I took it back to work and hand-delivered it to human resources. Then I returned to my office and grabbed my personal belongings, said goodbye to my beloved co-workers and walked away, passing my boss in the process, never saying a word to him."

Sandra was unemployed for two months and was then hired as the executive assistant to the president of a local non-profit. Myia did better as the change of environment was good for her. A year later she returned home and was enrolled in a private school with her brother.

After graduating from high school, Myia joined the Navy, got married, and had three children. Unfortunately, she passed away at the age of twenty-nine. "Her untimely death remains difficult, but I'll never regret that tough decision I made at a crucial moment in her development," Sandra said. "It was hard, very hard, but it had to be done and I was committed to getting her life on the right track at that time, even though I had to leave my job in the process. In the long term, it was clearly the right decision."

Whether as a parent or in the workplace, you have to make tough decisions at times. You have to stick with them. There will be scary moments. Just as Sandra questioned if she was doing the right thing, you will often be in a position where you are not sure what you are doing is right. But you have to be committed once you make the decision and sometimes you have to search deep into your heart and gut to know whether to pull the trigger. Sandra had the guts to make the decision to help her daughter and then remain committed to it.

On the other hand, what does this story tell us about her boss? He had a single parent trying to do the best she could with her two children. She followed policy in contacting him, yet he wouldn't call her back. He lost a good employee because he wasn't committed to his staff. You may have a staff member who is facing a tough personal situation. Be committed to getting to know your co-workers and employees. Make it a study of people! Sometimes you might have to live with short-term inconvenience as they handle personal matters, but in the long run, you will earn that person's trust and your team will benefit from it.

These situations aren't easy; they are where long-term thinking makes you successful. People make mistakes. You must have patience if you want a good employee for the long term. Patience takes toughness. Patience takes commitment.

* * * * *

Think about the successful businesses and organizations you know, or even the successful divisions or units in your organization. They probably achieved that success because they were committed to it from the leader on down through the division or unit. People who work there likely enjoy the peace of mind that comes from the self-satisfaction in knowing they did their best to become the best they are capable of becoming. It doesn't matter what the world thinks; if you are *committed* to something and it matters to you, that level of commitment is just as important as it is for people like Jeff Bezos, Serena Williams, LeBron James, Mary Barra, or Steve Jobs.

That's why the Chris Penzien example is so relevant. That match may not have mattered to anybody else, but it *mattered* to Chris. Years later, in 2016, I invited Chris back to speak to our student-athletes at Grand Valley State's annual Laker Pride and Tradition meeting, held during the first week of school at which we reviewed what we believed was important for them to know about being a student-athlete at Grand Valley. With Chris, I wanted our current student-athletes to know this skinny little guy helped catapult Grand Valley athletics to the proverbial next level with his hard work and commitment.

Even though he was never a coach or an athletics administrator for Grand Valley State, Chris Penzien, the number-two singles player on our third place Division II men's tennis team, was a rock star for Laker athletics. You can be too for your organization by showing the same level of commitment, even if you are lower on the organizational chart.

You never know what one play of commitment will lead to!

CONCLUSION

"It's not starting power that counts but staying power."

– John Savage

Y es, many people have starting power. They are all excited because they are involved in a new business or a new endeavor. At some point, the "newness" fades away. Finding true success is like that. True success stands the test of time. Any business or organization that can achieve success year-in and year-out over a good number of years meets that test versus the "one-hit wonders." Success in any endeavor is a problem-solving and decision-making process. One way to describe this is you have to go through the "hards" to get to the good times. That takes the glamour of success away in a hurry. Remember the fundamentals that will sustain you through the tough times, because there will be tough times. Stay focused on staying power.

Over the past thirty-five years, I've had the opportunity to make almost 300 speeches. In my very first one I focused on the fundamentals. I was finishing my junior year at Toledo. We had a very successful season that year. We won the Mid-American Conference and defeated Iowa in the first round of the NCAA Tournament before falling to Notre Dame in the Sweet Sixteen. Fayette (Ohio) High School Principal John Winzeler called and asked me to speak at their athletics banquet. I was honored and gladly accepted, and I'm thankful I did because it forced me to develop a philosophy for my life.

I was twenty-one years old and knew in one more year I would be heading into the "real world." I had to really think about what I wanted to become because I knew I didn't have a future playing basketball professionally. I was an education major and ended up being certified to teach math and physical education. I also knew I wanted to coach, and it was in my senior year of college when the seed was planted in my brain to someday become a collegiate director of athletics.

I was fortunate to have grown up in a home with wonderful parents. Ours was a Christian home. That upbringing, coupled with my constant participation in athletics, helped me develop my philosophy. I believe we are all blessed with certain God-given talents and abilities, and it's up to us to do the very best we can with those talents and abilities while on Earth. As a Christian, I strive to be the best Christian I can be, although I fall short often.

So what does it mean to do your best? To me, John Wooden's definition I've cited throughout this book says it best. If you can attain that "*peace of mind, which is a direct result of self-satisfaction in knowing you did your best to become the best you are capable of becoming,*" then you have done your best and have been a success.

I can tell you the exact moment I first recall experiencing this. It was after the final game of my collegiate basketball career. My senior year, during which I was a team captain, produced another great season, with us winning another Mid-American Conference title and advancing to the NCAA Tournament. Despite high expectations of advancing far in the postseason that year, we lost in the first round to Florida State.

Following the game, I was standing in the shower when it all hit me: I would never again play basketball competitively. As a kid, I was one of those gym rats that ate, slept, and drank hoops. I spent hours shooting baskets by myself to be good enough to obtain a college scholarship. I punished myself during my college years to be quick enough and strong enough to compete successfully in NCAA Division I basketball. And it all came to a screeching halt that night in March of 1980.

I'm not ashamed to admit I stood under the shower and cried my eyes out. I thought about all of the work and commitment I had put into the game of basketball. After several minutes, though, a peace came over me and I said to myself, "You got to be as good as you were ever going to get." Even though that was a loss, that moment positively influenced my approach to life greatly. From that point on, I put my playing career behind me and moved ahead as a teacher, coach, parent, administrator, and consultant. I'm certainly not perfect, but I have always genuinely tried to be the best I could be in each of these roles.

To be successful in any career field, you must find balance, surround yourself with talented people, teach others to share your vision of success, have the courage to take risks and overcome challenges, be positive about what you are doing and thankful for what you have, be unselfish in your pursuits, and commit to your goals and work hard.

I cannot tell you how often during my career when chaos seemed to be the order of the day that I would revert to these fundamentals. Sometimes it was to tell myself to slow down and find balance. Sometimes it was to tell myself I have good people around me, rely on them. Sometimes it was to tell myself to keep teaching. Sometimes it was to tell myself to have courage, you can do this. Sometimes it was smiling and staying positive despite the negativity around me. Sometimes it was to tell myself to keep doing things for others, plant seeds and good things will happen. Sometimes it was to just stay the course—be committed no matter what the circumstances.

And sometimes it was to tell myself to just make that one play, that one effort, because doing so consistently and intentionally will add collectively to success. *That's* what one play leads to.

These are the fundamentals of success I've found to be tried and true. Life is complicated, but achieving success doesn't have to be (KISS—keep it simple, stupid!). I hope they will help you be the best you can be. I hope they will help you achieve that "peace of mind, which is a direct result of self-satisfaction in knowing you did your best to become the best you are capable of becoming," and you will in turn help others achieve the same.

Now you know what one play will lead to!

ACKNOWLEDGMENTS

To all of the subjects whose stories, thoughts and beliefs appear in this book, thank you for making one play by sharing your stories and providing me the time and insight into your world. Hopefully your unselfishness will benefit others to help make their world a better place.

This book is based on a fundamental approach to one's endeavors of making just one play, because you never know what that one play will lead to. Thank you to my college coach, Bob Nichols, for teaching me and all of those who played for him this simple concept.

Thank you to Deb Bailey, who unfortunately lost her battle with cancer before the release of this book. She made many plays to make this world a better place and I appreciate the time I was able to spend with her. Deb was an amazing person and leader who leaves a lasting impact on her community. RIP, Deb.

To all of the people that have invited me to speak to their staffs or to a particular group of people of which they were responsible for providing a guest speaker, thank you all for allowing me to share my thoughts, which provided the foundation for this book!

Special thanks to Ritch Bentley and Jake Bentley of Five Count Publishing for allowing me to fulfill this dream of completing another book under your expert guidance and support. Kudos once again to my good friend Gary Brown for helping us shape the final product.

Last but not least, I have to thank God. As a Catholic Christian, I believe in Divine Guidance. The good Lord has brought some wonderful people into my life, as well as provided me with some wonderful experiences, and with this book I hope I have impacted the success of others.

ABOUT THE AUTHOR

The author of *Anchor Up: Competitive Greatness the Grand Valley Way*, Tim Selgo had a career of thirty-five years as a leader in college athletics as a coach and administrator. From 1996 to 2016, Selgo served as the director of athletics at Grand Valley State University, leading the Lakers in becoming the dominant athletics department in NCAA Division II.

Selgo has been inducted into three halls of fame; The University of Toledo Athletics Hall of Fame (2001), the Grand Rapids Sports Hall of Fame (2015), and the National Association of Collegiate Directors of Athletics (NACDA) Hall of Fame (2016).

Currently, after retiring from GVSU in July of 2016, Selgo is a consultant with Athletics Staffing & Consultants and an adjunct professor at Davenport University as well as a sought-after speaker on success and leadership.

Selgo and his wife Terry recently celebrated their thirty-seventh wedding anniversary. They have three children, Jennifer, Rachel, and Daniel, and five grandsons, Tray, RJ, Tucker, Henry, and Burke.